THE ORDER OF NATURE

THE ORDER OF NATURE

AN ESSAY

BY

LAWRENCE J. HENDERSON

 BOOKS FOR LIBRARIES PRESS

FREEPORT, NEW YORK

First Published 1917
Reprinted 1971

INTERNATIONAL STANDARD BOOK NUMBER:
0-8369-5699-0

LIBRARY OF CONGRESS CATALOG CARD NUMBER:
70-150186

PRINTED IN THE UNITED STATES OF AMERICA

PREFACE

" La nature est un ordre . . . dont l'ensemble constitue une puissance inaltérable dans son essence, assujettie dans tous ses actes, et constamment agissant sur toutes les parties de l'univers." . . . " un ordre . . . capable de donner successivement l'existence à tant d'êtres divers " . . . " cette puissance qui fait tant de choses, et qui cependant est constamment bornée à ne faire que celles-là."

LAMARCK, *Histoire naturelle des animaux sans vertèbres.*

THE study of adaptation, of which Lamarck is the great originator, has not yet won for itself a secure scientific foundation or led to clear and unequivocal interpretations of nature. Although the facts which this study presents are both universal and important, biologists have neither agreed upon their place in the theory of evolution nor discovered any principle by which they may be even unified.

This failure of our modern science is not hard to understand, and may fairly be attributed, in part at least, to the lack of a systematic study of *adaptability*; which at bottom is a physical and chemical problem, uncomplicated by the riddle of life.

For beneath all the organic structures and functions are the molecules and their activities. These it is that have been moulded by the process of evolution, and these no less have formed the environment.

I beg the reader to bear this in mind and constantly to remember one simple question: What are the physical and chemical origins of diversity among inorganic and organic things, and how shall the adaptability of matter and energy be described ? He may then see his way through all the difficulties which philosophical and biological thought have accumulated around a problem that in the final analysis belongs only to physical science, and at the end he will find a provisional answer to the question.

L. J. H.

CAMBRIDGE, MASSACHUSETTS,
March, 1916.

CONTENTS

v

THE ORDER OF NATURE

I

INTRODUCTION

MANY of the characteristics of inorganic nature, like the stability of the solar system and the enduring movements of the waters of the earth, are the very condition of existence for life as we know it and the source of diversity in organic evolution. This is perhaps one of the oldest interpretations of nature. But since Darwin's time the fitness of the environment has only occasionally aroused passing comment without ever entering the main current of scientific thought. And yet, whatever may be the final judgment of natural science upon either organic or inorganic harmonies, biological fitness is manifestly a mutual relationship. For, however present order may have developed out of past confusion, the organism and the environment each fits and is fitted by the other.

In a recent book [1] I have tried to recall attention to the many interesting peculiarities of the environment and to state the facts concerning the fitness of the inorganic world for life. This has turned out to be more notable and extensive than biologists had supposed, and more important in

---

[1] *The Fitness of the Environment.* New York, The Macmillan Co., 1913.

determining the universal characteristics of living organisms. The very nature of the cosmic process and of the physical and chemical phenomena of matter and energy bring about not only stability of the solar system, but very great stability of land and sea. Thus the temperature of the earth is more equable than it could be if the composition of the surface of the earth were other than it is. Thus the alkalinity of the ocean possesses a constancy which is nearly perfect, and this depends upon certain unique properties of carbonic acid. Thus the currents of the atmosphere and of the ocean, the fall of rain and the flow of streams are almost ideally regular, and are so only because water is different from any other substance.

Secondly, the properties of water cause a mobilization all over the earth of most of the chemical elements in very large quantities, and no other substance could so effectively accomplish this result. Once mobilized, these elements penetrate everywhere, borne by water, and the penetrating qualities of water are unique. In this manner the whole earth has become habitable.

Even more significant appear what the chemist calls the properties of the three elements, hydrogen, oxygen, and carbon, from which water and carbonic acid are formed. These are the most active of all elements (if we take account of both intensity and variety of activity), their compounds are the most numerous, the molecular structures which they form are incomparably the most complex and elaborate which have been brought to light. Moreover the energy which they yield in their mutual chemical transformations is more than other elements can provide, yet, because of their manifold reactions, more easy to regulate, to store, and to release.

In short the primary constituents of the environment, water and carbonic acid, the very substances which are placed upon a planet's surface by the blind forces of cosmic evolution, serve with maximum efficiency to make stable, durable, and complex, both the living thing itself and the world around it. With otherwise unattainable effectiveness they provide both matter and energy in many forms and in great abundance for growth and for repair, and in the ensemble of characteristics upon which these results depend they are unique. Nothing else could replace them in such respects, for their utility depends upon a *coincidence* of many peculiar and unequaled properties which they alone possess. | It is therefore certain that in abstract physical and chemical characteristics the actual environment is the fittest possible abode of life as we know it, so far as the elements of the periodic system are concerned. In truth fitness of the environment is quite as constant a component of a particular case of biological fitness as is fitness of

the organism, and fitness is quite as constantly
manifest in all the properties of water and carbonic
acid as in all the characteristics of living things.

Such a conclusion, however, only touches the
surface of the problem. For this relationship,
although mutual, is not symmetrical: it is something more than adaptation for it involves great
adaptability. In every case the particular characteristics of the organism fit a special environment, while the general physical and chemical
properties of water and carbonic acid fit the general
characteristics of life. But it may be shown that
stability, mobility, durability, complexity, and
availability of matter and energy are favorable not
merely to life as we know it; they are favorable to
any mechanism, to any possible kind of life in this
universe. For it is not by chance that life needs to
be stable, that it needs food, that it needs to be
complex if it is to evolve. Accordingly it is not for
any special or peculiar form of life, whether life as
we know it or another form, that this environment
is the fittest.

Just because life must exist in the universe, just
because the living thing must be made of matter in
space and actuated by energy in time, it is conditioned. In so far as this is a physical and chemical
world, life must manifest itself through more or less
complicated, more or less durable physico-chemical
systems.

Accordingly it is possible to assert and it will presently be demonstrated that the primary constituents of the environment are the fittest for those general characteristics of the organism which are imposed upon the organism by the general characteristics of the world itself; by the very nature of matter and energy, space and time. I feel sure that this conclusion is but a precise statement of a view that has long been vaguely held by many chemists.

The facts upon which this conclusion rests prove, I believe, that a hitherto unrecognized order exists among the properties of matter. For the peculiarities that make things what they are have been found not evenly distributed among the compounds of all the elements, nor in such manner as the laws of chance can explain, nor altogether in such manner as the periodic system of the elements describes. If the extreme values and unique properties be considered, very many are seen to belong to the three elements hydrogen, oxygen, and carbon in an arrangement that brings about stability of physical and chemical conditions, and diversity of phenomena, and, further, the possibility of the greatest complexity, durability, and activity of physico-chemical systems on the surface of a planet.

This order is masked when the properties of matter are considered statically. It becomes evident only when time is taken into account, for this is the order that determines the later course of cosmic evolution. At present it can be only imperfectly described, but there is reason to hope that a clearer description is attainable, and if an explanation seems to be beyond our grasp, the recognition of the order may yet serve a useful purpose by helping to define a little more clearly one of the riddles of existence.

Proceeding from the results of this earlier inquiry, I have, in the following pages, endeavored in a more rigorous manner to discuss the importance of the three elements for the process of cosmic evolution and by eliminating all biological theories and principles to rest the conclusions exclusively upon the secure foundation of abstract physical science. Such is the principal aim of the present essay.

But it has also seemed desirable at least to raise another question. For the fact cannot be escaped that these considerations have a philosophical as well as a scientific bearing. I have, therefore, after much hesitation, ventured to sketch the development of thought upon the problem of teleology, and at length to confront the scientific conclusions with the results of philosophical thought, in order finally to attempt a reconciliation.

I fear that this task has been accomplished with feeble strokes. It was not undertaken confidently, but in the sincere belief that when such questions are involved men of science can no longer shirk the responsibility of philosophical thought. Only thus can they hope to escape from many errors, like those that weaken both sides of the vitalistic and mechanistic controversy, and that do really retard the advancement of science. But in thus mingling philosophy with science a danger is incurred. I would, therefore, beg the reader still to remember after he has turned this page that, when all has been said, the scientific conclusions are independent of the philosophical problem of teleology. And — I wish to say it as clearly as possible — the present essay professes to demonstrate nothing but the existence of a new order among the properties of matter, and only to examine the teleological character of this order.

II

ARISTOTLE

The teleological appearance of nature and the
forms of life is a universal fact of human experience.
Hence it has been quite impossible for natural
science or philosophy permanently to ignore the
problem of teleology. Merely to explain away the
order of nature is no more satisfactory than to explain away matter itself. We may argue against
such ideas ever so ingeniously, but the experiences
of daily life steadily oppose the arguments, and
gradually overwhelm them. Thus men must always
inquire into the cause and significance of the teleological appearance of things. Efforts to solve such
questions are to be found in every system of
thought; they are greatly involved in the earliest
of all systems.

The peculiar philosophical standpoint of Aristotle, that position which enabled him to unify his
doctrine of the philosophy of nature, can only be
understood as the result of many different circumstances. And yet one feels that the teleological
parts of his thought were no mere accidents of time
and place. Aristotle's historical derivation from
Socrates and Plato, and, on the other hand, from
Greek physicians is important as a determinant of

his thought. Not less so are remote influences; for his work is continuous with the evolution of early science and primitive speculation. In short, both the sources of his system in personal experience, and its historical connections are to the point; and we may fairly think that they are often quite decisive in respect of his completed systematic views. But it is, above all other causes, his temperament, his native bent as a philosophical naturalist, to which the general character of his elementary teleological conceptions seems to be due. His system is only intelligible as an historical product, but on this subject his opinions are just his own.

No long reading of Aristotle's works is necessary to reveal in his general attitude toward final causes the very essence of his own mental disposition, the reflection of the world of life and thought as necessarily perceived through his eyes. Thus and not otherwise Aristotle was destined to see nature, if he was ever to see her as a whole, clearly.

Nevertheless, it was an historical accident that the systematic examination of the teleological concepts was first undertaken by Aristotle, and carried through under peculiar conditions and difficulties. The problem arose, to be sure, from his equal interest in the philosophy of forms and in natural history. Moreover, this conflicting interest in the end prevented a genuine resolution of the difficulties. But it was the accident of his time that compelled him to deal with the ideas of both Democritus and Plato. For the same reason he lacked a clear conception of mechanical or even of " efficient " causation, the one essential foundation of a clear theory of final causes. And, in turn, it was this defect which led to his peculiar idea of development, founded upon metaphysical concepts of matter and form. Hence his most highly elaborated considerations upon this point are least satisfactory.

In this view of development, which occupies the central position in the *Metaphysics*, one seeks in vain, I believe, for those elementary teleological conclusions which are so important in Aristotle's thought. They have disappeared in a subtle process of synthesis. It is true, contrary to the opinion of Gomperz,[1] that the modern idea of evolution, hence at least one question of objective science, is not entirely foreign to this analysis of development. The study of the *Politics* clearly establishes the point. But not in this concept of development, that concerns primarily the logical aspects of the idea of formation, nor in any similar speculations, does the riddle of the teleology of nature reveal itself simply and clearly. This can be grasped only in the scientific investigation of nature itself. Even so admirable a stroke as Aristotle's compari-

[1] *Greek Thinkers*, IV, 154. London, 1912.

son of natural formation with the work of the artist, whereby both analogies and differences are revealed, and the curious unimportance of conscious design is made evident, only confuses the real questions.

⤎ In the biological works, however, the teleological problems appear in their simplest forms. Even here there are difficulties and inconsistencies enough, and too many unlucky errors which count heavily in the later development of science. But the ideas are established; they arise as they are to recur for all later generations; and they initiate one of the great currents of human thought. Whatever blunders Aristotle may have made, he has here avoided fallacies that have proved dangerous to his successors, even in our own times. The reason for this success is that he adopts as his starting point those ideas which sooner or later must come home to every genuine naturalist. However they may be interpreted, these ideas will forever persist. They are the basis of all later speculations.

Aristotle was not equipped with the philosophical and scientific methods that have been found indispensable for a genuinely critical examination even of this simpler problem, and that are absolutely necessary for a formulation of the ultimate concepts. But his efforts, restricted in method though they had to be, were carried out

systematically and with great subtlety of dialectic;
they extended throughout the vast field of his
scientific knowledge; they especially involved the
whole of his favorite science of zoölogy; and the
result, accordingly, was not the least important of
his contributions to the understanding of nature.

Aristotle's discussion of causation arises from
the consideration that we are obliged to assign to
nature several different kinds of causation, two of
which are especially important for the philosophy
of science. He says himself: " The causes concerned in the generation of the works of nature are
. . . more than one. There is the final cause and
there is the motor cause. Now we must decide
which of these two causes comes first, which
second. Plainly, however, that cause is the first
which we call the final one. For this is the Reason,
and the Reason forms the starting point, alike in
the works of art and in the works of nature." [1] It
should be observed that the employment of but
two kinds of causation in the explanation of nature,
in place of the four which are to be found in his
more philosophical works, is characteristic of
Aristotle as a naturalist.

The relation between the two forms of causation
is not to be judged from the priority of the reason
alone for " it is plain . . . that both of these must,

[1] *De partibus animalium* (The Works of Aristotle translated into
English), I, 1, **639**ᵇ, 10–15. Oxford, 1911.

so far as possible, be taken into account in explaining the works of nature, or that at any rate an attempt must be made to include them both; and that those who fail in this tell us in reality nothing about nature." [1] Democritus, however, neglecting the final cause, reduces to necessity all the operations of nature; but though necessary, they are for a final cause, and for the sake of what is best in each case.

Thus it is also possible to understand, according to Aristotle, the failure of Empedocles, who was content to limit his reflections to mechanical causation. On the other hand, in the time of Socrates, men gave up inquiring into the works of nature, so that mechanical causation did not receive its due regard. The true method to be employed is illustrated by Aristotle as follows: " In dealing with respiration we must show that it takes place for such or such a final object; and we must also show that this and that part of the process is necessitated by this and that other stage of it." [2]

The study of physiology from this point of view is likely to lead to a vitalistic theory, but it hardly involves the general philosophy of nature. For Aristotle, however, the same considerations apply

---

[1] *De partibus animalium* (The Works of Aristotle translated into English, I, 1, **642**ª, 15. Oxford, 1911.

[2] *Ibid.*, 1, **642**ª, 30.

to the whole of nature. "Absence of haphazard and conduciveness of everything to an end are to be found in Nature's works in the highest degree, and the resultant end of her generations and combinations is a form of the beautiful." [1]

Teleology therefore appears to be a universal principle. In the science of life, however, a more subtle consideration arises, and this leads Aristotle to the concept of organization. "As every instrument and every bodily member subserves some partial end, that is to say, some special action, so the whole body must be destined to minister to some plenary sphere of action." [2]

"And the animal organism must be conceived after the similitude of a well-governed commonwealth. When order is once established in it there is no more need of a separate monarch to preside over each several task. The individuals each play their assigned part as it is ordered, and one thing follows another in its accustomed order. So in animals there is the same orderliness — nature taking the place of custom — and each part naturally doing his own work as nature has composed them. There is no need then of a soul in each part, but she resides in a kind of central governing place of the body, and the remaining parts live by

---

[1] *De partibus animalium* (The Works of Aristotle translated into English), I, 5, 645ᵃ, 20. Oxford, 1911.

[2] *Ibid.*, 645ᵇ, 10-15.

continuity of natural structure, and play the parts Nature would have them play." [1]

The idea of organization leads at once to a science of physiology based exclusively upon the concept of function. But once more a qualification arises; — this will not do as the complete science, for it deals only with final causes, accordingly " We have . . . to inquire whether necessity may not also have a share in the matter; and it must be admitted that these mutual relations could not from the very beginning have possibly been other than they are." [2]

Thus Aristotle arrives, no doubt less clearly than we may be inclined to think, at the conception of mechanism and teleology as complementary aspects of nature, which are always associated in its manifestations. And he is therefore led to a further question: " Let us now consider the character of the material nature whose necessary results have been made available by rational nature for a final cause." [3]

This no doubt is an important quest, which contemplates nothing less than the problem whose solution must put teleology in its proper place, or else eliminate it altogether. But the inquiry not unnaturally leads Aristotle from his general prin-

---

[1] *De motu animalium,* II, **703**ª, 30–35. Oxford, 1912.
[2] *De partibus animalium,* II, 1, **646**ᵇ, 25–30.
[3] *Ibid.,* III, 2, **663**ᵇ, 20.

ciples to the infinite complexity of phenomena; he
loses his clear vision of the principles, and stumbles
into pitfalls. For dysteleology is hardly less
obvious in nature than teleology, and the search
for a final cause of everything is a hopeless task.
Thus betrayed he concludes that: " . . . we must
not in all cases expect to find . . . a final cause;
for granted the existence in the body of this or that
constituent, with such and such properties, many
results must ensue merely as necessary consequences of these properties." [1] And he even dares
to be specific in his statement of this idea, that:
" Whenever things are not the product of Nature
working upon the animal kingdom as a whole, nor
yet characteristic of each separate kind, then none
of these things is such as it is or is so developed for
any final cause. The eye for instance exists for a
final cause, but it is not blue for a final cause unless
this condition be characteristic of the kind of
animal." [2]

Such ideas are damaging to the logical consistency of Aristotle's views. But they are harmless
to his science. Not so the complementary inconsistency. The explanation of natural phenomena
by final causes alone is at once incompatible with
his principles and destructive of all sound science.
Yet it is only too common in his scientific treatises.

[1] *De partibus animalium*, IV, 2, **677ᵃ**, 15.
[2] *De generatione animalium*, V, 1, **778ᵃ**, 30. Oxford, 1910.

We need make no difficulty of understanding Aristotle's perplexities on this point, for they depend upon his ignorance of the true manner in which mechanical processes are to be conceived. Thus for example the phenomena of the heavens were scientifically a complete riddle to him, and teleological explanations his only escape from perfect bewilderment.

It is singular that within a hundred years Archimedes and others should have been able to avoid these difficulties and, quite in the modern spirit, investigate the problems of mechanics. But for Aristotle this field of research was closed, and accordingly the use of final causes as a sufficient principle for the explanation of nature became usual in his works and the fatal defect of his natural philosophy.

It is unprofitable to continue the analysis of Aristotle's failures as a physical scientist. In certain departments these are too well known and too apparent to call for comment, but the blame for their perpetuation belongs to his successors. And it should never be forgotten that his great merits as a zoölogist more than offset his errors. We need not further consider his remarks upon teleology. For though other examples in great profusion could readily be cited, they add little to the essential considerations.

Accordingly, if the preceding analysis be not at fault, the foundations of Aristotle's teleology may be stated as follows: In the study of the living organism the mechanical cause and the reason of everything must both be sought. This is an absolute rule, although there is ground for the belief that sometimes the one explanation, sometimes the other, cannot be discovered.

The whole of nature is also subject to these two forms of causation. But the difficulties of the investigator are here multiplied. For on the one hand matter is a refractory medium; it does not lend itself quite perfectly to the working out of the ends of nature. For this reason results may sometimes arise which are due to necessity and not properly to final causes at all. On the other hand the wider our experience and knowledge of nature, the more often do we lose track of the chain of necessary causation and discover only the final causes.

It is only reasonable to proceed one step further in the elimination of the unessential from Aristotle's views. We then reach the heart of his doctrine: Teleology and mechanism are in all phenomena, for they are complementary aspects of all things and all changes. Every qualification of this view is evidently due to Aristotle's perplexities as a naturalist or physicist. Therefore, it is the task of the investigator to " consider the character of the material nature whose necessary results have been made available by rational nature for a final cause." A more pregnant statement was never uttered.

One special view remains to be noted: the conception of the living thing as an autonomous unit in which every part is functionally related to every other and exists as the servant of the whole. No external end or purpose guides this being. Here, as in the state, the teleological principle is within. Every activity is subject to the regulative control of the soul. But, in the biological treatises, the soul is nothing more than a name for the principle of autonomy. Kant and the modern physiologists have expanded this view without improving it. It is the complete formulation of the biological principle of organization.

III

THE SEVENTEENTH CENTURY

DURING the next two thousand years the history of teleology more than of other things is a record of the stagnation and decay of thought. Although the great achievements of Archimedes and the Alexandrians did almost at once afford an example of how unnecessary is a regard for teleology in the development of physical science, the lesson remained unheeded, and in the course of time the system of Aristotle won the commanding position in all domains of thought.

The followers of Aristotle, Mohammedans and Christians alike, were able in most respects only to degrade his doctrine, for they had lost his spirit of independence; only rarely could they comprehend the precision of his abstractions and generalizations; and above all they were too far from nature. Perhaps, of all his works, the teleological portions suffered most at their hands. The rare independent spirits who from time to time arose — Roger Bacon, Nicholas of Cusa, Leonardo da Vinci — failed or did not try to shake the authority of the schools, and meanwhile the practice of explaining the phenomena of nature by their supposed final causes, alone increased and developed. Under the

influence of logical pedantry or the belief in authority, now arrayed in the service of theology, Aristotle's worst faults were perpetuated, and when
the currents of modern thought began to flow, the
abuse of ideas which were admirable in their in-
ception had long been complete.

The actual situation is revealed in the works of
Francis Bacon. When only thirteen years old his
mind had revolted against the accepted doctrines
and the mature philosopher was not slow to detect
and define the sources of error. These are first
stated in a famous passage of " The Advancement
of Learning."

" The second part of Metaphysic is the inquiry
of *final* causes, which I am moved to report not as
omitted, but as misplaced. And yet if it were but
a fault in order, I would not speak of it; for order
is matter of illustration, but pertaineth not to the
substance of sciences: but this misplacing hath
caused a deficience, or at least a great inproficience
in the sciences themselves. For the handling of
final causes mixed with the rest in physical inquiries, hath intercepted the severe and diligent
inquiry of all real and physical causes, and given
men the occasion to stay upon these satisfactory
and specious causes, to the great arrest and prejudice of further discovery. For this I find done
not only by Plato, who ever anchoreth upon that
shore, but by Aristotle, Galen, and others, which

do usually likewise fall upon these flats of *discoursing causes.* For to say that *the hairs of the eyelids are for a quickset and fence about the sight;* or that *the firmness of the skins and hides of living creatures is to defend them from the extremities of heat or cold;* or that *the bones are for the columns or beams, whereupon the frames of the bodies of living creatures are built;* or that *the leaves of trees are for protecting of the fruit;* or that *the clouds are for watering of the earth;* or that *the solidness of the earth is for the station and mansion of living creatures*, and the like, is well enquired and collected in Metaphysic; but in Physic they are impertinent. Nay, they are indeed but remoras and hindrances to stay and slug the ship from further sailing, and have brought this to pass, that the search of the Physical Causes hath been neglected and passed in silence. And therefore the natural philosophy of Democritus and some others, who did not suppose a mind or reason in the frame of things, but attributed *the form thereof able to maintain itself to infinite essays or proofs of nature*, which they term *fortune*, seemeth to me (as far as I can judge by the recital and fragments which remain unto us) in particularities of physical causes more real and better enquired than that of Aristotle and Plato; whereof both intermingled final causes, the one as a part of theology, and the other as a part of logic, which were the favourite studies respectively of both

those persons. Not because those final causes are
not true, and worthy to be enquired, being kept
within their own province; but because their ex-
cursions into the limits of physical causes hath bred
a vastness and solitude in that track. For otherwise keeping their precincts and borders, men are
extremely deceived if they think there is an enmity
or repugnancy at all between them. For the cause
rendered, that *the hairs about the eye-lids are for the
safeguard of the sight*, doth not impugn the cause
rendered, that *pilosity is incident to orifices of
moisture; Muscosi fontes* [the mossy springs], etc.
Nor the cause rendered, that *the firmness of hides
is for the armour of the body again against extremities of heat and cold*, doth not impugn the cause
rendered, that *contraction of pores is incident to the
outwardest parts, in regard of their adjacence to
foreign or unlike bodies;* and so of the rest: both
causes being true and compatible, the one declaring
an intention, the other a consequence only. Neither
doth this call in question or derogate from divine
providence, but highly confirm and exalt it. For
as in civil actions he is the greater and deeper poli-
tique, that can make other men the instruments of
his will and ends and yet never acquaint them with
his purpose, so as they shall do it and yet not know
what they do, than he that imparteth his meaning
to those he employeth; so is the wisdom of God
more admirable, when nature intendeth one thing

and providence draweth forth another, than if he had communicated to particular creatures and motions the characters and impressions of his providence." [1]

It is apparent that Bacon does not differ radically from Aristotle. Had he been able to distinguish the original elements of Aristotle's thought from the master's blunders and the school's vagaries, he must have dealt with the problem quite differently. But neither the age nor the cast of Bacon's own mind was favorable to historical criticism.

Perhaps for this reason Bacon's one genuine contribution to the teleological problem is to be found in his discussion of the method of science. Admitting the Aristotelian principle that mechanism and teleology appear to be two complementary aspects of things, he showed that experience demands their separation in scientific research. Thus he discovered the peculiar feature of physical science that it must proceed as if final causes did not exist, even though he fully agreed that they may be conceived as real. In other words physical science can recognize only one kind of causation, which is physical causation. This is a return to Democritus and Empedocles.

Bacon's criticism is quite sound, but it misses that important feature of Aristotle's thought, the

---

[1] *The Philosophical Works of Francis Bacon*, pp. 96, 97. London, Routledge, 1905.

concept of organization. And yet this concept had undergone important developments at the hands of Aquinas. Perhaps the defect is fortunate; for certain it is that physiology needs sound physical investigations quite as much as physics itself. But the defect remains, and it is significant of Aristotle's superiority as a naturalist.

In another respect Bacon and Aristotle suffer from a like disability. Neither is able to conceive just how one should go about a physical research. A modern philosopher, to be sure, is far better informed upon this subject, for history affords him many more examples, and Bacon's misconceptions now seem almost inexcusable. Nevertheless he is notoriously wide of the mark in his illustrations of scientific method in the *Novum Organum*, and he failed to see the point of much contemporary research. Perhaps one direct influence of his thought concerning the subject of causation was to enlighten his immediate successors, if indeed the more clear-sighted were in need of enlightenment, but it is certain that he had no valid notion of mechanical causation. This first arises in the investigations of Galileo and receives its first critical treatment at the hands of Descartes.[1]

The ancients, however, did not wholly lack an idea of mechanical causation, although it finds no

[1] For an excellent and learned discussion of the development of the concept of causation see E. Meyerson, *Identité et Realité*. Paris, 1908.

place in the thought of Aristotle. Very imperfectly the old atomic theory served the purpose, and the speculations of Lucretius provided a foundation for the conception of the indestructibility of matter,[1] or even perhaps of the conservation of mass.[2] The same idea was destined to find a place in Newton's inquiries,[3] and we may note in passing that, for scholastic philosophy, causes had likewise been things or substances, rather than forces or conditions.

In accordance with this atomic view of things, that which results from a change is such as it is because it has been formed without gain or loss of substance from that which has disappeared. These ideas, however, were always vague. There can be no doubt that, if they proved themselves impotent in the chemistry of the eighteenth century until Lavoisier introduced them into his experimental researches, they must have been without permanent influence of a sufficiently definite nature upon the thought of earlier times.

In fact the development of dynamics rather than of chemistry equipped the scientific investigator with his earliest representation of the true character of mechanical necessity. This concept arises directly from the principle of inertia, and therefore

[1] *De natura rerum*, 1, I, 150, 486–487, 500, 552–565, 584–598.

[2] *Ibid.*, 361–363.

[3] *Opticks*, 3d ed., p. 375.

from Galileo's experiments on falling bodies.[1] Long before its definite formulation by Galileo it was grasped by Descartes, perhaps independently,[2] and incorporated in his philosophical system. Thereby the defect in Bacon's formulation of the method of science was temporarily repaired.

For Descartes, struggling with his new philosophical system, the principle of inertia leads directly to the law of conservation of movement, his " memorable error " as it was called by Leibniz.[3] Accordingly Descartes proceeds from the hypothesis that the product of mass by velocity in all natural phenomena is constant, to the formulation of a principle of universal necessary causation. From his reflections upon the principles of dynamics he was led to the belief that " God never changes his manner of acting — and in order to maintain things with the same action and the same laws which he has caused to obtain in their creation, it is necessary that he should now conserve in them all the movement which he then introduced into them, together with the property which he has given to this movement that it shall not forever remain attached to the same portions of matter, but in their encounters shall pass from one portion

[1] On the idea of inertia in antiquity, see P. Tannery, *Revue générale des sciences*, xii, 1901, 333.

[2] Meyerson, *loc. cit.*, p. 104.

[3] *Mathematische Schriften*, ed. Gerhardt, VI, 117. See also below, pp. 33, 36.

to another." [1] This is Descartes's first contribution to the definition of the teleological problem. In spite of the unsound foundation, it marks a very great advance in thought.

The argument, however, leads him much farther, and in his progress he becomes the founder of the systematic view, long since developed as the basis of dynamics and, in a manner, of all natural science, that every phenomenon is ultimately reducible to matter and motion. He arrives at a consideration of the functions of the living organism. And at one stroke, aided by Harvey's researches upon the circulation, he founds the mechanistic theory of the vital processes. Here too it would seem that mechanical causation must be supreme; but this conclusion is incompatible with the theological view of voluntary action.

Thus arises, for the first time clearly defined, the ever-perplexing problem of vitalism. The chains of mechanical causation may be rigorously determined, but where living things are involved they can never seem so. Yet Descartes himself was not inextricably entangled in this difficulty, from which no later thinker has been able to escape. The very errors of his dynamics, which reduce his conception of causation to a mere preliminary sketch of the true principle, left him a way out. Such is the origin of his mistaken notion that the

[1] *Principia*, Part II, ch. 42.

will might operate by changing not the quantity but merely the direction of motion. The theory is ingenious and undoubtedly fills a real want, as many analogous speculations of a later date attest. But it could not withstand the most superficial analysis and it soon fell before the rapid advance of theoretical mechanics.

All the other contributions of Descartes to the teleological problem may be summed up in one statement. He, more clearly and systematically than any of his predecessors, perceived and elucidated the complementary relation of mechanism and teleology, thereby reinforcing Aristotle's position. For him all things are teleological at all stages of their necessary development because they originally possessed a teleological character which is itself necessarily conserved. This view, his valuable though imperfect discussion of causation, his mechanistic theory of physiological activity, and his definition of the vitalistic hypothesis in the discussion of freedom, determine Descartes's position. I have given no account of his admirable analysis of the problems and his clear exposition of the concepts. In his case, apart from theological interests and such considerations as involve the properties of matter, these may justly be taken for granted.

The philosophical system of Descartes moves chiefly in another world from that of these simple ideas. For that very reason we need not here investigate the subject. Even his strange metaphysical conceptions of matter and extension are without importance for his theory of mechanical causation, because derivative from this and from his other scientific views. In the thought of Descartes, as in that of Aristotle in an earlier day, and of Leibniz a little later, philosophical principles are not to be regarded as consistent with scientific principles. The effort is to be scientific, yet in all three systems the philosophical principles are derived from a number of incompatible sources, of which the scientific is probably most important. But physical science and its mathematical foundations seem to have been Descartes's central interests, and the source of a great part of what is truly original in his philosophy.[1]

No long succession of centuries was to pass before the fallacies of the Cartesian theory of causation were revealed, for they had been published to a world seething as never before with scientific thought, and busy with the experimental and mathematical investigation of dynamics. Huygens, Newton, and Leibniz immediately took up the task which Galileo and Descartes laid down. And very soon, with the aid of many lesser workers and thinkers, they had completed the definition of

[1] Cf. Gilson, *La doctrine cartesienne de la liberté et la théologie.* Alcan, Paris, 1913.

the scientific principles and improved the idea of mechanical causation.

Leibniz's attack upon the Cartesian dynamics has been often discussed, but not always with a clear understanding of the true nature of the underlying scientific principles.[1] There is not much of originality in the criticism itself, which is largely founded upon the results of Huygens and others. The one point which concerns the teleological problem is a demonstration that the direction of motion cannot be altered by the action of the will, since the conservative principle in respect of *vis viva* must apply, if at all, to the sum of moving force in any direction. With this demonstration the peculiar vitalism of Descartes, which had already received its death blow at the hands of his disciple Geulincx [2] passes out of the history of thought.

The great interest of Leibniz's position is due to the fact that he first faced the problem which inevitably arises from a philosophical examination of the completed principles of classical dynamics. His treatment of the subject reveals all the capacity of his admirable intellect, and the result is a synthesis of the thought of his century. In grasp of all departments of knowledge and speculation, in skill of dialectic, and in sheer intellectual power it is one of the great examples of philosophical

[1] See Mach, *Die Mechanik*, 3d ed., p. 274.
[2] Windelband, *Geschichte der Philosophie*, 3d ed., p. 341.

analysis. But it suffers from the fatal defect of a constant concern for the interests of theology. It tries to serve two masters. Leibniz could not but believe that mechanical necessity is a principle without exceptions, and accordingly that God " foresaw and arranged everything once for all." [1] The doctrine is developed as a result of his principle of the conservation of *vis viva* (the conservation of $\Sigma \, m \, v^2$) though there is reason to believe that it really arises, as in an imperfect form it had occurred to Descartes, more or less directly out of the idea of inertia. For, historically speaking, the idea of absolute universal determinism seems to be almost necessarily imposed upon the student of dynamics. He may think to derive it from the principle of the conservation of motion, of *vis viva*, or of energy, or from the two principles of thermodynamics together; the psycho-physical riddle may lead him to all sorts of ingenious subtle qualifications; but the idea always stands in his mind as the generalization of his concept of causation or as a self-evident *a priori* principle from which the notion of cause is itself derived. No doubt, however, the principle is not strictly an *a priori* judgment, in that it cannot be formed with the necessary precision in the absence of extensive scientific knowledge. Therefore the simplest view is to regard it as a necessary corollary of the

---

[1] Ed. Gerhardt, III, p. 400.

concept of inertia,[1] upon the assumption that all phenomena may be reduced to matter and motion. In this connection we may recall Newton's first law of motion; " Every body continues in its state of rest or of uniform motion in a straight line unless compelled to change that state by forces impressed upon it."

Leibniz is certainly the real author of the conviction that every phenomenon, without any exception whatever, is the result of mechanical causation and is therefore rigorously and unequivocally determined. The view is almost as old as thought itself, and was very widely held in his day. But Leibniz founded it upon a careful analysis of the known laws of nature, and thus made it directly accessible to the understanding and imagination. His analysis has been criticized, extended, and thereby gradually modified. But throughout the later development of scientific thought it has never for a moment lost the support of the greater number of qualified judges, and today it constitutes the first article of the orthodox scientific creed. The fact is historically interesting that Leibniz conceived visible motion of masses as somehow losing itself in that of the imperceptible constituent particles, when motion apparently ceases. The identity of this excellent guess with our modern theories is obvious.

[1] But see Meyerson, *loc. cit.*

The position of Leibniz is made quite clear by many passages in his works, of which one may suffice as an example. In the *Monadology* he declares that " Descartes saw that souls cannot at all impart force to bodies, because there is always the same quantity of force in matter. Yet, he thought that the soul could change the direction of bodies. This was, however, because at that time the law of nature, which affirms also the conservation of the same total direction in the motion of matter, was not known. If he had known that law, he would have fallen upon my system of Pre-established Harmony.

" According to this system bodies act as if (to suppose the impossible) there were no souls at all." [1] . . .

Leibniz might better have treated the problem which thus arises in the simple Aristotelian manner. Two considerations, apparently, led him far beyond the purely destructive criticism of the Cartesian position to his theory of Pre-established Harmony. These are the perplexing riddle of voluntary action and the interests of theology. It has become customary, at least in scientific circles, to look upon the monad, which is at the very foundation of Leibniz's Pre-established Harmony, as a vague creation of fancy, incoherent, unintelli-

---

[1] *Monadology*, 80, 81, in Leibniz trans. by Montgomery. Chicago, 1908, p. 269.

gible, even preposterous, and quite unworthy of the mind of one of the inventors of the calculus. It is not so. Mr. Bertrand Russell has a right to be heard on this point, and he declares that: "This seemingly fantastic system could be deduced from a few simple premises, which, but for the conclusions which Leibniz had drawn from them, many, if not most, philosophers would have been willing to admit." [1]

There can be no doubt, however, that this unique example of metaphysical speculation according to the pattern of mathematics does not concern us. It has no importance for the history of the formation of current teleological concepts, in so far as I find them relevant to our problem.[2] The *Monadology*, to be sure, is nothing if not teleological, and it was designed to be so. But the permanently significant teleological elements are not involved in the fate of the whole structure. This may be overthrown without including them in the destruction. Only one of these concerns the present subject, and this is present in all of Leibniz's speculations. For him, as for Aristotle, the universe is no less teleological than mechanical. But Leibniz, even more than Descartes, is compelled to put the

---

[1] *A Critical Exposition of the Philosophy of Leibniz*, p. viii. Cambridge, 1900.

[2] Cf. however Ward, *The Realm of Ends: Pluralism and Theism.* Cambridge, 1911. Lecture III, etc.

origin of the teleological back of all mechanism at the origin of things, and thus in the creation itself. There can never be any genuine teleological novelties of whatever origin, for all is order. Even miracles are in accordance with the order of nature, just as Babbage later crudely explained.

Details of Leibniz's speculations may appear to contradict or gravely to qualify his fundamental position, but such vagaries are not more important than the bewilderment of Aristotle under similar conditions. For Leibniz resembled both Descartes and Aristotle especially in this, that his scientific views are fundamental, his philosophical opinions largely secondary.[1] Especially that which is original and valuable in the philosophy of Leibniz is of scientific origin, for the results of science and mathematics were the only novel sources of his speculations.

The necessity of assimilating the idea of absolute mechanical determinism to his metaphysical position had one other important result in Leibniz's thought. It led to an examination of the problem of organization. The investigations of the seventeenth century biologists had gradually revived interest in this question, and at length it had become possible vaguely to perceive how different is the problem of organization itself from

[1] Cf. B. Russell, *op. cit.;* Couturat, *La logique de Leibniz.* Paris, Alcan, 1901; Cassirer, *Leibniz's System,* Berlin, 1902.

that of simple purposeful behavior. Not only the vitalism of Descartes, but the far wider view of Stahl, which extends the animistic principle from the operation of consciousness to the organism as a whole, appear to Leibniz as radically false. For him nothing in the living being is heterogeneous with mechanism, and everything has its mechanical cause or explanation. Otherwise, as the modern mechanists still contend, it must be quite unintelligible. But the organism is a mechanism of exquisite perfection where everything takes place as if the materialistic philosophy of Epicurus and Hobbes were true. Yet this absolute scientific truth possesses only relative philosophical validity. The mechanical character of the organism, like that of nature itself, is just the means by which we attain to the eternal truths. And in the organism we can readily see the philosophical limitations of the mechanical description as an ultimate philosophical position. "Therefore, every organic body of a living being is a kind of divine machine, or natural automaton, infinitely surpassing all artificial automatons. Because a machine constructed by man's skill is not a machine in each of its parts; for instance, the teeth of a brass wheel have parts or bits which to us are not artificial products, and contain nothing in themselves to show the use to which the wheel was destined in the machine. The machines of nature, however, that is to say, living bodies, are still machines in their smallest parts *ad infinitum*. Such is the difference between nature and art, that is to say, between divine art and ours." [1] Leibniz's conception of organization is thus inferior to Aristotle's.[2] In spite of this he has established the important principle that organization is compatible with mechanism.

So far as it concerns the development of the theories of teleology the result of the first period of modern science and philosophy is now apparent. Very important is the strengthening of Aristotle's original position. Mechanism and teleology are still to be regarded as complementary aspects of all things, whether physical or biological. The peculiar character of the living being as an organism is still recognized, but, without the help of Aristotle's profound insight and in the absence of advanced biological thought, vaguely conceived. Meanwhile nature itself has put on more and more the appearance of the organism. On the other hand, the mechanistic has been logically disentangled from the teleological. All is as if mechanism were the only ultimate reality, or at least all phenomena of matter and motion are so. And all phenomena are reducible to matter and motion. Newton, no less than Leibniz, seems to take this for granted.

---

[1] *Monadology*, 64, *op. cit.*, pp. 265, 266.

[2] Above, p. 16.

Moreover all phenomena of matter and motion are necessarily determined according to that concept of conservation which is the direct consequence of the idea of inertia.

Hence teleological principles are involved only in the *interpretation* of phenomena, especially in the interpretation of nature as a whole and of the organism. This interpretation, however, involves a form of description, which, though quite independent of ordinary physical description, is once more correlative with it. Final causes, therefore, remain in high favor. In physical science they have lost their power to do mischief. But in wider fields of thought they are quite as dangerous as ever.

IV

THE EIGHTEENTH CENTURY

IT is a dismal period that followed the deaths of
Leibniz and Newton. Taking the lead which they
had given, physical science went on its way un-
troubled by further metaphysical problems save
those of its own creation. But meanwhile the
philosophy of nature degenerated into eighteenth
century Theism, and so departed altogether from
the road of progress. And yet, in spite of appearances, the field was not quite free for childish play
with final causes. Those who were so engaged
might suppose that they could find their full justification in the philosophy of Leibniz and in the
evolution of Theology. Gradually, however, the
ideas of Locke, most independent of seventeenth
century philosophers, were working in another
direction, and at length Hume arose. By this time
the teleological question had come to be regarded
as identical with the problem of design; a view for
which little can be said except that it reveals the
development of a vague conception of organic
unity in nature. In every other respect it is a sign
of decadence.

Hume's historical position no less than his
natural temperament was ideally favorable to the

task of examining the problem of design. In the history of the subject this is a rare combination, but necessary for unbiased judgment. After Aristotle he was perhaps the first notable thinker again to approach teleology in a thoroughly dispassionate and impartial spirit. Not that he was indifferent, as so many have believed, to the influence of his thought on morals, but he evidently possessed the true philosopher's conviction of the supreme value of thought itself. And whatever concern he may have felt for his destructive influence upon religion in general must have been offset by the desire to overthrow the abhorred theological system of his day.

Design was the great and primary question of the time in Hume's England, from which he could not have escaped. It is very evident, however, that he would not if he could, for he has himself reported with favor the view that natural theology should come as the mature climax of the other philosophical studies.[1]

It is probable that Hume's *Dialogues concerning Natural Religion* may justly be regarded as his last word in philosophy. Chronologically the latest of his philosophical writings, their style marks them as the product of much labor and careful recon-

[1] " That students of philosophy ought first to learn Logics, then Ethics, next Physics, last of all, of the nature of the Gods. *Chrysippus apud Plut. de repug. Stoicorum.*" *Dialogues concerning Natural Religion*, Edinburgh and London, 1907, pp. 6, 7.

sideration. We know too that, during the long
period when they remained unpublished, he sought
the criticisms of his friends; [1] and he reserved the
publication until after his death.

In forming a true opinion of the *Dialogues* two
other considerations are important. On the one
hand, Hume lived in a day when the echoes of the
seventeenth century scientific revolution had,
especially in England, almost died away. A period
of quiet and continuous progress had ensued,
which, except for Lavoisier's great innovation, was
to continue almost undisturbed for many decades.
For this reason, no doubt, science and mathematics
have but a small place in Hume's thought, so that
his famous discussion of causation is according to
the scientific view one-sided and sterile. On the
other hand, Hume was almost equally isolated in
the history of philosophy. He is so far removed
from the philosophers of the seventeenth century
that his works are on the whole, notably in respect
of the teleological problems, discontinuous with
theirs. And he did not live to see that great result
of his own labors; Kant " wakened from his dogmatic slumbers."

There are difficulties in discovering Hume's real
opinions beneath the uncertain conclusions of the
Dialogues concerning Natural Religion. At the very
outset, in an interesting apology for this literary

[1] *Loc. cit.*, p. ix.

form,[1] he has himself indicated that his views are not quite established on many of the questions at issue, indeed the *Dialogues* may fairly be taken as a demonstration that these problems surpass human power, and it is known that he was dissatisfied with the results of his analysis.[2] But the general tendency of the argument is not doubtful.

For Hume there can be but one foundation of a belief in design. This is the recognition of natural order, which, directly apprehended, is enough. There is, in the last analysis, no need of argument on the point, for the conviction of design arises without process of logic. As he makes Cleanthes say: " The order and arrangement of nature, the curious adjustment of final causes, the plain use and intention of every part and organ; all these bespeak in the clearest language an intelligent cause or author. The heavens and the earth join in the same testimony: The whole chorus of Nature raises one hymn to the praises of its creator: You alone, or almost alone, disturb this general harmony. You start abstruse doubts, cavils, and objections: You ask me, what is the cause of this cause ? I know not; I care not; that concerns not me. I have found a Deity; and here I stop my enquiry. Let those go farther, who are wiser or more enterprising.

[1] *Loc. cit.*, p. 2.   [2] *Ibid.*, p. xi.

" I pretend to be neither, replied Philo: and for that very reason, I should never perhaps have attempted to go so far; especially when I am sensible, that I must at last be contented to sit down with the same answer, which, without farther trouble, might have satisfied me from the beginning." [1]

"A purpose, an intention, a design strikes everywhere the most careless, the most stupid thinker; and no man can be so hardened in absurd systems, as at all times to reject it." [2]

But this is Hume's only concession to natural theology. Unlike the bitterly conscientious Butler, he can find no place for evil in this field of thought, and thus expresses himself: "And is it possible, Cleanthes, said Philo, that after all these reflections, and infinitely more, which might be suggested, you can still persevere in your Anthropomorphism, and assert the moral attributes of the Deity, his justice, benevolence, mercy, and rectitude, to be of the same nature with these virtues in human creatures ? His power we allow infinite: whatever he wills is executed: but neither man nor any other animal is happy: therefore he does not will their happiness. His wisdom is infinite: he is never mistaken in choosing the means to any end: but the course of nature tends not to human or animal felicity: therefore it is not

[1] *Loc. cit.*, pp. 70, 71.   [2] *Ibid.*, p. 165.

established for that purpose. Through the whole compass of human knowledge, there are no inferences more certain and infallible than these. In what respect, then, do his benevolence and mercy resemble the benevolence and mercy of men ?

" Epicurus's old questions are yet unanswered.

" Is he willing to prevent evil, but not able ? then is he impotent. Is he able, but not willing ? then is he malevolent. Is he both able and willing ? whence then is evil ? " [1] This is by no means a fair treatment of the problem of evil, but it is sufficient as a reply to the theology of the day.

For Hume, such considerations destroy the whole fabric of natural theology,[2] and leave nothing but that impression which the recognition of the order of nature produces on the mind. The analysis reveals his firm conviction that the human reason is entirely unqualified for thought upon the subject. In like manner the pre-established harmony of Leibniz loses its whole foundation because it, too, denies human misery, or at least loses sight of it altogether.[3]

After many other discussions a final conclusion upon design is undeniably reached, and very carefully formulated as follows:

[1] *Loc. cit.*, pp. 133, 134.
[2] Other departments of theological thought are not here in question.
[3] *Ibid.*, p. 125.

" If the whole of Natural Theology, as some people seem to maintain, resolves itself into one simple, though somewhat ambiguous, at least undefined proposition, *That the cause or causes of order in the universe probably bear some remote analogy to human intelligence:* If this proposition be not capable of extension, variation, or more particular explication: If it afford no inference that affects human life, or can be the source of any action or forbearance: And if the analogy, imperfect as it is, can be carried no farther than to the human intelligence; and cannot be transferred, with any appearance of probability, to the other qualities of the mind: If this really be the case, what can the most inquisitive, contemplative, and religious man do more than give a plain, philosophical assent to the proposition, as often as it occurs; and believe that the arguments, on which it is established, exceed the objections, which lie against it ? " [1]

It is but a step from this position to Kant's theory that all teleological conclusions are mere reflective judgments of the human mind. But the historical importance of Hume's criticism is chiefly due to his destruction of all claims of natural theology to a scientific or philosophical standing. The natural theologians, indeed, went on for nearly another century, still working over

[1] *Loc. cit.*, pp. 189, 190.

the genuine results of science into the semblance of
a theological form. But they did so only by
ignoring all that Hume had told them, and with
rare exceptions, their labors have nothing more to
do with the real thought of the race.

Yet the teleological problem remains. Theism
had quite unwarrantably injected an anthropo-
morphic element into teleology, but it had not
altered the appearance of order. And nothing was
farther from Hume's mind than to deny the existence of this. He does, however, analyze it, and in
the analysis are to be found his positive contributions to the problem.

It is apparent to Hume that the mind can conceive certain states of a blind chaotic system, arising by chance in the course of time, which must
maintain themselves for a longer or shorter period
and must, therefore, present the appearance of
order. He states his thought as follows: " Is there
a system, an order, an oeconomy of things, by
which matter can preserve that perpetual agita-
tion, which seems essential to it, and yet maintain a
constancy in the forms, which it produces ? There
certainly is such an oeconomy: for this is actually
the case with the present world. The continual motion of matter, therefore, in less than infinite trans-
positions, must produce this oeconomy or order;
and by its very nature, that order, when once
established, supports itself, for many ages, if not

to eternity. But wherever matter is so poised, arranged, and adjusted as to continue in perpetual motion, and yet preserve a constancy in the forms, its situation must, of necessity, have all the same appearance of art and contrivance, which we observe at present. All the parts of each form must have a relation to each other, and to the whole: and the whole itself must have a relation to the other parts of the universe. . . ." [1]

Such an origin and development of the universe might well account, even when we take the living being itself into consideration, for the appearance of order and our resulting impression of design. In fact, says Hume, "It is in vain, . . . to insist upon the uses of the parts in animals or vegetables and their curious adjustment to each other. I would fain know how an animal could subsist, unless its parts were so adjusted ? " [2]

This, if not the principle of the survival of the fittest, is at least the principle of the survival of the fit. Properly speaking it is even closer to Darwin's thought, for the positive fact in both ideas is the elimination of the unfit. Another aspect of Darwin's conception of evolution is clearly developed by Hume in an analysis of the conditions which have governed the evolution of the ship, by a process of trial and error in which human skill and foresight had but small part. In truth the underlying idea

[1] *Loc. cit.*, pp. 105, 106.   [2] *Ibid.*, p. 109.

in all these considerations leads to a general statement of that tendency toward dynamic equilibrium which is one of the principles of modern physics and biology alike. Science has hardly succeeded in formulating the view as broadly as Hume states it. But Hume's position is none the less well founded.

This theory, though not entirely original with Hume, marks an important advance in the development of thought.[1] It clearly demonstrates the manner in which we are to conceive a mechanistic universe at work upon the production of something very like organic unity. I am of the opinion that it also shows Kant's view that teleology is exclusively a function of the reflective judgment to be untenable, or at least unimportant for natural science.

[1] Cf. " But in what ways yon concourse of matter founded earth and heaven and the deeps of the sea, the courses of sun and moon, I will next in order describe. For verily not by design did the first-beginnings of things station themselves each in its right place by keen-sighted intelligence, nor did they bargain sooth to say what motions each should assume, but because the first-beginnings of things many in number in many ways impelled by blows for infinite ages back and kept in motion by their own weights have been wont to be carried along and to unite in all manner of ways and thoroughly to test every kind of production possible by their mutual combinations, therefore it is that spread abroad through great time after trying unions and motions of every kind they at length meet together in those masses which suddenly brought together become often the rudiments of great things, of earth, sea and heaven and the race of living things." Lucretius: " On the Nature of Things," translated by H. A. J. Munro, London (no date), Routledge & Sons, p. 163.

There is another consideration, developed at an earlier stage of Hume's discussion, to which these conclusions lead back. The sceptic Philo is made to say that, " For aught we can know *a priori*, matter may contain the source or spring of order originally, within itself, as well as mind does. . . ." [1]

Thus the original Aristotelian position once more reappears. But in this later form it is so developed and refined as to become almost a scientific problem. For we may fairly ask what is the nature of this original source or spring of order. The problem might even be solved if we could but construct Laplace's world formula, since the various quantities therein contained and the functional relations which must obtain between them would provide all the data that could be necessary. In other words, the *form* of the equation would provide a complete description of the source of order in the world. The question would then arise whether there is any teleological significance in the original properties and arrangement of matter or if perchance the tendency to equilibrium alone is teleological, as seems to be the view of extreme scientific materialism. I think there can be no doubt that Hume's conclusions are hostile to the latter opinion.

Hume's discussion of teleology is in many respects decisive. It still remains, for the man of

[1] *Loc. cit.*, p. 36.

science, on the whole the best treatment of the subject, for it is clear, specific, and single-minded. Once for all it eliminates dogmatic theology, and in several particulars it provides Kant with the material for his reëxamination of the problem, according to his peculiar critical method. All this is due not so much to the novelty of Hume's thought as to an illumination which proceeds from his lucidity, his thoroughness, and, above all, his perfect honesty. Descartes had been lucid and Leibniz thorough, each had brought to the task a better mathematical and scientific equipment than Hume's, but neither had attained to that spiritual freedom which permits the single-minded search for truth.

It is important that until the last half of the eighteenth century there is no effort to separate the philosophical interpretations from the scientific results in investigating the problem of natural teleology. Science had long since won its independence, which had been demanded by Bacon and declared by Newton, himself a thorough teleologist. But there was no suspicion that the teleological problem might perhaps be regarded as exclusively philosophical. This is true in spite of the fact that mechanics was well understood to be concerned in its investigations with mechanical causation alone. The only way to get rid of the teleological in science had been to deny the exist-

ence of teleology. To this condition Kant under-
took to put an end.

The *Kritik der Urteilskraft* contains Kant's ripest
and most complete critical examination of teleology. In his view the belief that teleological forms
and combinations exist in nature may be regarded
as an aid, when the principle of mechanical causation is insufficient, in reducing phenomena to rules.
Such a standpoint, however, is an affair of the reflective judgment, and does not concern physical
science. Now this manner of studying phenomena, which according to Kant cannot be regarded as the business of physics at all, has had
very important results in our attitude toward
nature. " For in the very necessity of that which
is purposive, and is constituted just as if it were
designedly intended for our use, — but at the same
time seems to belong originally to the being of
things without any reference to our use, — lies the
ground of our great admiration of nature. . . .[1] "

Yet such ideas can justify a belief in the external
purposiveness of nature only if we believe that
which they serve, for instance mankind, to be itself
a purpose of nature. Kant, therefore, concludes:
" Since that can never be completely determined
by mere contemplation of nature, it follows that
relative purposiveness, although it hypothetically
gives indications of natural purposes, yet justifies

[1] Kant's *Kritik of Judgment*, trans. Bernard, London, 1892, p. 264.

no absolute teleological judgment." [1] Thus the ox needs grass, and man the ox. But we do not see why the existence of man is necessary.

Aristotle's conception of organization presents a different case, for here the teleology is internal, or as Kant prefers to put it, a living being is " both cause and effect of itself." [2] " Every part not only exists *by means of* the other parts, but is thought of as existing *for the sake of* the others and the whole." [3] Moreover, unlike all machines, the organism possesses formative power as well as mechanism.

In Kant's opinion, if the organic products of nature are only imperfectly analogous to the products of art, on the one hand, they are, on the other hand, hardly more analogous to the organization of nature as a whole. Therefore the teleology of the living organism and of nature as a whole are both unique, and the conclusion is inevitable that organic beings alone can be regarded as absolute purposes of nature. For all other apparent purposes in nature are merely relative. Therefore it is only through the organism that the concept of teleology is necessarily forced upon us. This concept, however, naturally leads to the view of collective nature as a teleological system. In this system mechanism is regarded as the servant of reason and nothing is worthless or in vain.

[1] *Loc. cit.*, p. 271.   [2] *Ibid.*, p. 274.   [3] *Ibid.*, p. 277.

" It is plain that this is not a principle for the determinant but only for the reflective judgment; that it is regulative and not constitutive; and that we derive from it a clue by which we consider natural things in reference to an already given ground of determination according to a new law-abiding order; and extend our natural science according to a different principle, viz., that of final causes, but yet without prejudice to the principle of mechanical causality. Furthermore, it is in no wise thus decided, whether anything of which we judge by this principle, is a *designed* purpose of nature. . . .[1] " " We venture to judge that things belong to a system of purposes, which yet do not (either in themselves or in their purposive relations) necessitate our seeking for any principle of their possibility beyond the mechanism of causes working blindly. For the first Idea, as concerns its ground, already brings us beyond the world of sense; since the unity of the supersensible principle must be regarded as valid in this way not merely for certain species of natural beings, but for the whole of nature as a system." [2] " Natural characteristics which demonstrate themselves *a priori*, and consequently admit of insight into their possibility from universal principles without any admixture of experience, although they carry with them a technical purposiveness, yet cannot,

[1] *Loc. cit.*, p. 285.   [2] *Ibid.*, p. 287.

because they are absolutely necessary, be referred to the Teleology of nature, as to a method belonging to Physic for solving its problems. . . . Even if they deserve to be brought into consideration in the universal theory of the purposiveness of things of nature, yet they belong to another [science], i. e. Metaphysic, and constitute no internal principle of natural science; as with the empirical laws of natural purposes in organized beings, it is not only permissible but unavoidable to use the teleological *mode of judging* as a principle of the doctrine of nature in regard to a particular class of its objects." [1]

After these characteristic critical delimitations of his subject Kant at length reaches the position that we speak of the teleology of nature *as if* it were designed, but with the understanding that no design, in the proper meaning of the word, is involved. Thus ends the first division of the *Kritik of Teleological Judgment*.

He now turns to the *Dialectic* of teleological judgment which opens with the two maxims of judgment: " All production of material things and their forms must be judged to be possible according to merely mechanical laws " and " Some products of material nature cannot be judged to be possible according to merely mechanical laws. (To judge them requires quite a different law of causality,

[1] *Loc. cit.*, p. 289.

namely, that of final causes)." [1]   Turned into
objective principles these two maxims are in his
opinion clearly contradictory, and one must be
false.   But as mere maxims of judgment he
declares that they involve no contradiction in
fact.

Regarded as an objective principle the final
cause can have no place in Kant's philosophy for
the reason that a thing as a natural purpose is
objectively inexplicable. " That it is not suscep-
tible of proof is clear from the fact that as concept
of a *natural product* it embraces in itself necessity and at the same time a contingency of the
form of the Object (in reference to the mere laws of
nature) in the selfsame thing regarded as purpose.
Hence, if there is to be no contradiction here it
must contain a ground for the possibility of the
thing in nature, and also a ground of the possibility
of this nature itself and of its reference to something which, not being empirically cognizable
nature (supersensible), is therefore for us not
cognizable at all." [2] Or, more concretely stated,
" How can I number among the products of nature
things which are definitely accounted products of
divine art, when it is just the incapacity of nature
to produce such things according to its own laws
that made it necessary to invoke a cause different
from it ? " [3]

[1] *Loc. cit.*, p. 294.   [2] *Ibid.*, pp. 307, 308.   [3] *Ibid.*, p. 309.

According to Kant, therefore, the most complete teleology could prove at best nothing more than that the human understanding cannot conceive a world such as ours otherwise than as the product of a supreme cause operating designedly. But he believes that we are driven into this same position even by our restricted teleological conclusions. This view, identical with Hume's, is finally formulated as follows: " We cannot otherwise think and make comprehensible the purposiveness which must lie at the bottom of our cognition of the internal possibility of many natural things, than by representing it and the world in general as a product of an intelligent cause." [1]

To the vulgar such a conclusion may seem barren enough, not so to Kant, who with unwonted enthusiasm passes on to one of his most famous remarks: " It is indeed quite certain that we cannot adequately cognize, much less explain, organized beings and their internal possibility, according to mere mechanical principles of nature; and we can say boldly it is alike certain that it is absurd for men to make any such attempt or to hope that another *Newton* will arise in the future, who shall make comprehensible by us the production of a blade of grass according to natural laws which no design has ordered." [2] Those who have mistaken Darwin for the Newton of the blade of

---

[1] *Loc. cit.*, p. 312.   [2] *Ibid.*, pp. 312, 313.

grass strangely misconceive Kant's meaning, though not, I think, in all respects.

The general conclusion of the *Dialectic* may perhaps be summed up as follows: Reason must not for a moment overlook the mechanistic principle. For our knowledge of nature is not at all advanced by explanation according to final causes, in that we can never know their teleological mode of action. But on the other hand we must never lose sight of the teleological. For this would make reason fantastic, just as a merely teleological view makes it visionary. Yet the two principles of mechanical and teleological causation cannot be united. Though complementary, and in no proper sense contradictory, they are independent in such a manner that one method of explanation excludes the other. In short, they are heterogeneous; their assimilation in one principle can occur only in the supersensible; and regarding this we can form no determinate conception, for the principle is transcendent.

The organism presents peculiar difficulties. Human understanding is quite powerless to conceive the existence of the phenomena of organization as a result of mere mechanical causation. Yet we must not on that account even here attempt to decide against the mechanical principle. For upon the assumption that such things are teleologically determined, we are still compelled to conceive them as mechanically produced. And, when we do so conceive them, we necessarily put aside the teleological explanation altogether. This argument, which has lost none of its force, is the true mechanistic reply to all vitalistic theories.

Finally it is to be observed that we can never hope to determine how much mechanism does for the development of the teleological in nature, but rather must seek the mechanical and the teleological in all things. And this is the reply to blind mechanism.

Unquestionably these results, important as they are in the philosophical controversies of the biological theorists, may be regarded as unimportant for natural science itself. Kant has accorded to mechanical causation all that the most thoroughgoing man of science can ask for it — unless the scientist should turn philosopher. But science had already usurped such rights. At the most Kant merely legalized an accomplished fact.

The real purpose of the discussion seems to be to secure a like independence for the teleological principle. This Kant tries to accomplish by removing teleology altogether from the field of the determinant to that of the reflective judgment. Here he hopes to establish it in perfect security. But here it must remain in isolation, fenced off from natural science by the critical philosophy itself. Yet even metaphysical fences often suffer from the tooth of time. And it is very doubtful if at this point Kant's undertaking has been philosophically successful. For who shall say that the periodic system of the elements or the second law of thermodynamics is the concern of the determinant rather than of the reflective judgment? Indeed the reverse is clearly the case. Yet no argument can ever remove such principles from natural science.

Further, the fully developed hypothesis of natural selection appears to involve mechanism and teleology in a new entanglement, unforeseen by Kant's analysis and inconsistent with it. Thus he declares that nothing is gained for the theory of nature or the mechanical explanation of its phenomena by means of its effective causes, by considering them as connected according to the relation of purposes. And yet without such consideration the idea of natural selection could never have arisen, for only the teleological judgment tells us that such things as adaptations exist and we can only prove them to be mechanical products after we have become aware of their existence. According to Kant's view the development of existing organic forms into new shapes must always be judged to result from the purpose that is within them and conformably to it. In such a view there is no place for the natural selection of random variations.

A vague conception of mechanistic evolution is, however, not unknown to Kant's penetrating mind,[1] and he meets the difficulty by pushing back the origin of the teleological to an earlier period, quite after the manner of Leibniz and many others. Thus he arrives at pre-established harmony, as applied to organic evolution, and, as a means of representing evolution, at Blumenbach's views on the theory of epigenesis. But just as there is no room in his view for the development of adaptations through the operation of unaided chance, so *a fortiori* spontaneous generation is out of place: " That crude matter should have originally formed itself according to mechanical laws, that life should have sprung from the nature of what is lifeless, that matter should have been able to dispose itself into the form of a self-maintaining purposiveness — this he [Blumenbach] rightly declares to be contradictory to Reason." [2]

Throughout the whole course of the essay Kant struggles hard but in vain to convert his concept of universal teleology into a more synthetic view which shall somehow represent the whole of nature under the guise of an organism. At last he abandons the attempt and turns, where we need not follow him, to man and human affairs.

Such, so far as I understand it, is the substance of this famous work. I have set it forth, not be-

---

[1] *Loc. cit.*, p. 338.   [2] *Ibid.*, pp. 345, 346.

cause it seems to be important for the present purpose, but because I wanted a justification for passing it by. Kant has indeed revealed to us the human understanding at work upon the problems of mechanism and teleology. He has enabled us to be self-conscious in this difficult task. But in every other respect he has left the question just where Hume left it. From the problem of the teleology of nature design is eliminated, and with it theology. Organization remains. Universal teleology remains. And both have a tendency, as science advances, to recede to the very origin of things.

Science has never paid much attention to Kant's speculations concerning the judgment. It disregards the metaphysical distinction between the determinant and the reflective judgment, just as it disregards the metaphysical distinction between space and time, on the one hand, and matter and energy, on the other. Admitting that these may be valid discriminations concerning the operations of the reason, the scientist takes his reason, just as he takes his own sensory apparatus, for granted.

The conclusion at which Kant arrives is nothing but the metaphysical formulation, according to the peculiar principles of his critical philosophy, of a distinction between mechanical and teleological explanations which Aristotle, Bacon, and Kant's other great predecessors had with varying success sought to grasp. I have no doubt that it may be regarded as a genuine metaphysical discovery. Yet from time immemorial a vague realization of this distinction has governed actual scientific research. Since the seventeenth century there has never been a question of mingling the teleological judgment with the researches of physical science. A sign of this development of scientific method may be found in the pious Newton's rigorous exclusion of all reference to final causes from the *Principia*. The concluding scholium, " On the eternal deity by and through whom the universe exists," which was added to the second edition, reinforces this point. Further, in his first rule of reasoning in philosophy, Newton declares that we are not to assume more causes than are sufficient and necessary for the explanation of the observed facts.[1] This rule was, I think, not formulated in order to exclude final causes, but it could have been thus stated only by one who disregarded them as a matter of course. Thus, even in Kant's day genuine physical science, as distinguished from the spurious natural theology, could have no interest in such speculations, for it had long since forgotten final causes quite as completely as had mathematics itself.

In biology there is hardly an enduring trace of Kant's influence. The concept of function,

---

[1] *Principia*, Thomson & Blackburn's edition. Glasgow, 1871, p. 387.

naïvely held as a guide in research, has weathered all storms. The physiologist in his laboratory neither thinks nor cares whether the idea is an affair of the reflective judgment. As a rule functions raise in his mind no more philosophical doubts than energy or the electric current. He simply goes on investigating them. Thus, to be sure, he is applying Kant's precepts, for all his investigations are rigorously physical and chemical, but he is quite indifferent to any such considerations. He stands with Harvey; his determinism, almost without exception, is that of Leibniz; and for him judgment is so little suggestive of metaphysics that, in English, it represents sagacity rather than one of the elementary constituents of human reason. Here, as in physical science, the earlier vague distinction, not the refined product of Kant's metaphysics, determines the course of events.

More important than these well known characteristics of scientific research, as a means to the appraisal of Kant's influence, is another fact. It will be remembered that when Leibniz asserted it, the principle of absolute mechanical causation became established. In truth no assertion of the principle was really necessary to its establishment, for it was already implied in the principles of dynamics, and it is undoubtedly an inevitable tendency of the mind.[1] But though mechanical causation

---

[1] Meyerson, *loc. cit.*

can readily be abstracted from all teleological
views, teleological forms, as Kant thoroughly
explained, always involve chains of mechanical
causation. For this reason Kant has been powerless to do what Leibniz did. Though we can
readily separate the mechanical from the teleological in nature, we can on no account separate the
teleological from the mechanical, if we are to think
about it scientifically. So, in spite of Kant, when
scientific research employs teleological concepts
such as function, adaptation, fitness, or natural
selection, it is obliged to regard them as cognate
with mechanism. And I believe that organization
has finally become a category which stands beside
those of matter and energy.

If this be so Kant's whole position has been
judged and condemned. The fact is that for science
the idea of organization, like that of energy, becomes established through a process of induction.
It is today a component part of the theoretical description of nature, unique indeed, yet thoroughly
homogeneous with the other elements of that
description. In short, at the one point where teleological concepts have always been inevitable,
modern natural science holds fast the view which
it owes to Aristotle in his rôle of biologist, undisturbed by the criticisms of Kant. This destructive
task of science is completed by the establishment of
principles such as those of Carnot and Mendeleeff

above mentioned, which are at once the work of the reflective judgment, according to Kant's analysis, and by common consent integral parts of physical science.

V

BIOLOGY

HISTORICALLY the most striking result of Kant's labors was the rapid separation of the thinkers of his own nation and, though less completely, of the world, into two parties; — the philosophers and the scientists. No doubt this was an inevitable stage in the movement of thought. But it could hardly have come to pass so definitely without the influence of the systems of the philosophers of nature and of Hegel, both of which are Kantian in origin. The consequent reaction of science against metaphysics was extreme, and has of course had certain unfortunate effects. But even though somewhat uncritical, it was on the whole well justified and certainly most beneficial to the progress of natural science in the middle period of the nineteenth century. For the time the work of philosophy in discovering concepts and assigning to them their rôle as regulative principles in scientific research was done. Accordingly the history of science in the nineteenth century bears few traces, and those chiefly of an early date, which point to philosophical influence.

Especially the problem of teleology had received a philosophical treatment quite adequate to the needs of the contemporary scientific investigator. He was licensed to postulate absolute mechanical determinism throughout nature. On that basis he was quite free to study all things from the standpoint of physical science. But yet, he was told, organization is a concept from which the biologist has no escape, and this can be *thought* only with the help of ideas which are teleological and not mechanical. That which is organized, the structure, the process, is indeed exclusively mechanical, but like the idea of beauty, the idea of organization is in no sense a mechanical concept. Finally there is that in the universe, we know not what, which leads all men, the most devout and the most materialistic alike, to speak of nature. This too can on no account interfere with the business of science. And yet it points to a remote possibility that we may some day find in the universe a clue which shall lead us to think of nature as a whole somewhat as we now think of the organism. I have put these ideas in a modern form so that they may be more clearly intelligible. But they were all accessible to the men of a hundred years ago.

There was also philosophical ground, though no doubt quite unnecessary and uncalled for, to justify the scientific study of the development of that which we regard as teleological. Kant had allowed this only with important reservations, but Hume had admitted none upon the subject.

Under the circumstances, we may proceed to the examination of the fate of these ideas in the scientific history of the nineteenth century without regard to the independent history of philosophy, especially of German philosophy. In France and England no such complete hostility was ever established between the scientists and the philosophers, for the scientists of these countries had no bitter memories of bondage under the rule of metaphysics. Accordingly English and French philosophers are more closely related to nineteenth century science. Of course this depends very largely upon the fact that they did not as a rule, especially early in the century, adopt the views and methods of German idealism. In the end a few of the results of Hegel's speculation and other products of the German school must be considered. They have finally found a place in our present analysis of the teleological problem, as it presents itself to the natural scientist. But these need not be treated in their historical development.

Until Lotze's time there is no further association of science with German philosophy. Lotze returned to a position which is nearly identical with that of Leibniz, though the establishment of the principles of thermodynamics had modified his manner of conceiving mechanical determination. He first established friendly relations with science by founding a criticism of the despised philosophy of nature upon the basis of broad and profound scientific learning, especially in the medical sciences. He then turned to the teleological concepts and reëxplained them to a generation of investigators who had not themselves taken the trouble to analyze problems from which they could not escape. But Lotze was a somewhat isolated figure of his day, and though he influenced a number of superior minds, he established no easily recognized current of thought. Indeed, so far as the elements of the teleological problem are concerned, he said nothing very new.

A more important influence than the German philosophers was Goethe, who stands far above any of Kant's successors in wisdom and an almost instinctive recognition of the truth. As a philosophical poet of nature he was long, though not permanently, to hold the German people to a view of nature as teleological, a view which has in it something of the true spirit of the Renaissance. His scientific activities were also important. For in judgment he surpassed his scientific contemporaries like Humboldt almost as much as in philosophical intuition he surpassed Schelling. Thus in Germany at least, where the philosophical influences have failed, Goethe's unsystematic views have had a wide influence. This has been much needed, for among Goethe's countrymen the fantastic excesses of materialism have quite equalled the visionary excesses of idealism.

On the whole neither Goethe nor Lotze, nor indeed Mill, Spencer, or Comte, seriously modified the development of scientific thought, which now becomes our principal concern.

Needless to say what is chiefly involved is the progress of biology. In the nineteenth century the concept of organization appears for the first time as an explicit postulate of scientific research.

There has never been a period when the idea of function was absent from physiological investigation. And it would be an almost hopeless task to trace the transformation of this idea, with widening experience, into the larger one of organization. Provisionally, it may therefore suffice to note the conscious and deliberate use of the latter idea in " Cuvier's Law." According to this hypothesis it is possible after a careful study of any one part of an animal, for example a tooth, to reconstruct the whole. Nothing could correspond more perfectly with Aristotle's original position concerning the organic relation between the parts and the whole.

This hypothesis is to be regarded as an induction from the necessary method of paleontology. Although untenable as a strict and universal principle, it is well grounded in Cuvier's own paleontological studies and in the vast fabric of his comparative anatomy. Cuvier, however, was a life-long opponent of the theory of evolution. He failed, therefore, to represent his idea in its true light as a necessary implication of the historical continuity of the forms of life. In this later aspect it has done good service in one of the principal fields of research developed by the Darwinian theories, and thus it has never ceased to be a constant preoccupation of biology. In this special form the idea of organization dominates all modern biology.

Physiology was more deliberate in setting up the principle, because organic activity is harder to define and to describe. At least as early as the time of Johannes Müller the idea was clearly grasped.[1] But not until the establishment of experimental morphology did it become overtly a guiding principle of physiological research. One very important influence toward this result is to be found in the speculations of von Baer. He was, however, less concerned with the larger questions than with an examination of the simple concept of teleology as a necessary component of scientific thought. For him the *teleophobia* of his scientific contemporaries is a mere vulgar prejudice which rests upon the old mistaken notion that somehow the teleological view interferes with the mechanical explanation. He is convinced that " All necessity and compulsion in nature lead to ends, and all

[1] Du Bois-Reymond, *Reden*, ii, p. 217.

tendency to ends is accomplished solely through necessity and compulsion." [1] The fundamental difficulty of his contemporaries is therefore that they do not understand the thought of their predecessors, Aristotle, Bacon, Descartes, and Leibniz. This, in its simplest form, he adopts.

But a further difficulty is involved in the terminology of the German language. The word *zweckmässig* says too much, for it puts into *teleological* the idea of purpose or conscious design. And this von Baer as a man of science cannot allow. He, therefore, coins the term *zielstrebig*. For the recognition of ends in nature is no less certain to him, even as a man of science, than is that of conscious purpose illusory. This position, radically anti-Kantian, is formulated as follows: " I cannot help expressing the conviction that scientific research, in that it establishes the existence of harmony among the different forces of nature, does and should lead us to the recognition of a general and ultimate principle (*Urgrund*) thereof." [2] It is interesting to observe that Hegel had long since reached a similar view.[3]

In some respects these opinions of von Baer have not received the general approval of men of science. But they have greatly supported the teleological

[1] v. Baer, *Reden*, ii, p. 234.

[2] *Ibid.*, ii, p. 77.

[3] Cf. J. S. Haldane: *Mechanism, Life and Personality*. London, 1913.

point of view in physiology, for his name is a great
one in the foundation of modern biology.

These positions being established, von Baer
turns to the problem of organization, and fully
expounds the necessary concepts. It is curious
that he should seem to attach less importance to
this idea than to that of *Zielstrebigkeit*. Perhaps he
did not see how useful the larger concept could be
in research. Nevertheless the truly Aristotelian
idea of internal teleology of the organism is at the
bottom of his biological philosophy.[1] He and
Bichat are the first of the *organicists*.[2] Their suc-
cessor is Claude Bernard. This great man, whose
purely mechanistic researches stand at the foundation of many departments of physiology, steadily
exerted all his influence in favor of the idea of
organization. He recognized a directive and
organizing idea in the animal, and again and again
insisted upon it.[3] Yet his analysis of the problem,
like that of von Baer, was not complete. Though
he, like all other physiologists, employed the idea
of functional activity as a guide in research, though
he was fully aware of Cuvier's method in paleontology, his just concern for the integrity of physio-

[1] *Loc. cit.*, ii, p. 188.

[2] It is hardly correct to derive them, as M. Delage has done, from
Descartes. (*L'Hérédité*, p. 408.) Their descent is clearly from Aristotle; their modification of his view the necessary result of modern
physical theories.

[3] *Introduction à la médicine expérimentale*, p. 162.

logical method beguiled him into declaring that " The metaphysical evolutive force by which we may characterize life is useless in science, because, existing apart from physical forces, it can exercise no influence upon them." [1]

This, strange to say, is Kant's own error. It is as if one should declare that the idea of the periodic system of the elements is useless to science, because, existing apart from the physical forces, it can exercise no influence upon them. What Claude Bernard well knew, but failed here to point out, is that organization, like the second law of thermodynamics, is a condition of those physico-chemical phenomena which were the subject of his investigations. At times, however, he stated the case more correctly.

During the later years of von Baer and Claude Bernard, the ideas of Darwin were accomplishing a revolution in general biology. Not the least important result was at least temporarily to establish adaptations as the most positive of realities. Yet an adaptation is only to be defined in terms of organization. In the orthodox Darwinian view it is that which contributes to the preservation of the whole. There is nothing in its merely physical character which enables us to recognize it as an adaptation. Only its function reveals its true nature.

[1] *La science expérimentale*, 3ème ed., p. 211.

In the course of time some of Darwin's original positions have been weakened and the more extreme views of his followers overthrown. As a result this manner of thinking about adaptation is somewhat out of fashion. But it endured quite long enough to leave its mark upon several departments of the science. And it is very doubtful if any one will be bold enough ever again to put aside the idea of function itself or to deny its necessary implications.

Meanwhile a number of independent lines of investigation have developed from Darwin's researches. One of the most interesting of these is the study of experimental morphology initiated by Professor Wilhelm Roux. This subject appears to have developed, partly at least, as the realization of a program of research founded upon Roux's quasi-philosophical analysis of the characteristics of life.[1]

Such a process is a genuine curiosity in the history of science. According to Roux the living being may be defined as a natural object which possesses the following nine characteristic autonomous activities: Autonomous change, autonomous excretion, autonomous ingestion, autonomous assimilation, autonomous growth, autonomous movement, autonomous multiplication, autonomous transmission of hereditary characteristics, and autonomous development. This conception, as Roux

---

[1] *Der Kampf der Teile im Organismus.* Leipzig, 1881.

admits, is closely related to Herbert Spencer's famous conception of life as " The continuous adjustment of internal relations to external relations." [1] Roux's discussion of the subject was independent of Spencer's influence and, in its specification of conditions, his analysis possesses certain advantages over the English philosopher's more abstract statement. But, from the standpoint of physical science, it is gravely deficient in method and has never been regarded as more than a preliminary statement of the several physiological aspects of the fact of organization.

What has given Roux's investigation its value and influence is that there is thus presented a provisional discrimination of organic activities as a basis for the experimental physiological study of organization itself. Thus regarded, Roux's service to biology may be seen to be both permanent and important. With the foundation of experimental morphology the problem of organization assumes its proper place in physiological research. The experimental results of the new science clearly prove that the place is secure.

This department of science has developed independently, and only in recent years can its influence upon the older science of physiology be detected. The physiologists, in their more abstract and more analytical researches, have usually dealt

---

[1] *Principles of Biology,* revised edition, 1909, p. 123.

exclusively with physical and chemical phenomena. Unlike Roux's followers, they have been concerned with those things which are organized in the living being, rather than with the organization of them. Their very method of research, which proceeds from a preliminary analysis of the factors of organization, has obscured the larger biological problem.

At length Pavlov's researches on the glands of digestion, the study of internal secretions and hormones, Sherrington's investigation of the integrative action of the nervous system,[1] Cannon's study of the emotions,[2] and many other independent lines of investigation have cleared the ground, and at the present moment the physico-chemical treatment of the problem of organization is widely if somewhat vaguely recognized as the ultimate goal of physiological research.[3]

In the study of metabolism, which has also had an independent development, the idea of organization has long dominated research. This is due to the fact that here the concept of equilibrium cannot be avoided. At an early period in the history of the science it was discovered that a normal organism is in a state of nitrogen equilibrium. That is to say, the composition, in respect of compounds

[1] New York, 1906.   [2] *Ibid.*, 1915.

[3] Cf. *Mechanism, Life and Personality,* J. S. Haldane, London, 1913, and my review, *Science,* N. S. xlii, 378.

of nitrogen, is steadily preserved, through the regulation of a long chain of most intricate chemical processes. Day by day the ingestion of nitrogen is approximately equal to the excretion. A modification of the diet may cause a temporary disturbance of the condition, but this is soon restored. The phenomena of growth and disease are found to involve more enduring changes. Hereupon, by a process of reasoning patterned upon that of physical science, growth is declared to involve nothing more than other phenomena superimposed upon the underlying conditions, thereby modifying the observed facts in such manner that the fundamental state is partly obscured. And disease is after all, in its very essence, a disturbance of organization; in short, diseases of metabolism involve by definition disturbances of equilibria, which may or may not be compensated.

Further research reveals similar equilibria concerning carbon, sulphur, phosphorus and the other elements. The results are extended to definite chemical compounds such as water, salt, sodium bicarbonate, glucose, and the like. It is perceived that the equilibria of temperature, of osmotic pressure, of alkalinity, which involve physico-chemical states rather than chemical substances, are truly analogous phenomena.

Meanwhile it has always been clear that within certain limits the existence of these equilibria is essential to the preservation of life itself, and that they might have been taken for granted. The real question has been to define the normal and pathological fluctuations, their duration, their limits, and their relations to other phenomena. In short, so far as these problems are concerned, the study of metabolism has consisted in an attempt to describe as thoroughly as may be, and if possible to explain, the fluctuations of the approximately constant physical and chemical conditions of the body. In other words, the task of the investigator has been to make known the facts concerning the *regulation* of the ultimate physical and chemical constitution of the organism. In this undertaking he has always kept in mind the idea that the organism exists in a state of dynamic equilibrium, just as it was long ago conceived by Cuvier.

Now this idea of regulation, so familiar in the investigations of the temperature of the body, and in many other general problems of metabolism, is the very concept to which all the other independent investigations of organization as a physiological problem also lead. Thus Roux has long since declared, and recently reasserted [1] the belief, that the capacity of autonomous regulation of all nine of his elementary characteristics is quite the most important of all the peculiarities of life. For example, this is what makes possible the direct

[1] *Die Selbstregulation*, Halle, 1914.

adaptation to the environment, or, in other words, the acquiring of characteristics. In like manner the action of hormones, the integrating function of the nervous system, and the phenomena of emotional excitement investigated by Cannon are all regulatory.

It is now possible to see that Herbert Spencer's conception of life as " the continuous adjustment of internal relations to external relations," though doubtless far from satisfactory as a characterization of life itself, is really a true statement of the phenomena of organization. Vague though it may be, it is confirmed by the results of experimental morphology, of physiology, and of the science of metabolism.

I should be sorry to produce the impression that this idea of regulation is well defined in general physiology. The fact is that current views upon the subject are very generally loose and perhaps in part contradictory. But it is certainly rigorously defined in some departments of the science. And it is unquestionably everywhere in use.

Perhaps the most convenient definition of regulation is Driesch's: " We shall understand by regulation any occurrence or group of occurrences in a living organism which takes place after any disturbance of its organization or normal functional state, and which leads to a reappearance of this organization or this state, or at least to an approach thereto." [1] This statement bears the mark of having been formulated for the purposes of experimental morphology, and accordingly lacks the quantitative character that one finds in the investigations of physico-chemical regulations, such as temperature. It will, however, suffice to establish the point that the concept of regulation is governed by that of organization.

Thus, at length, Aristotle's original view of the internal teleology of the living thing, which is nothing more than self-regulation, has completely established itself in physiology.

Meantime still another development of biological research, the study of animal behavior, which is an offshoot of psychology, has undertaken the task of systematically examining the phenomena of organization as they appear in the integrated activities of the individual.

Among the investigations which have contributed to the establishment of the principles of regulation and organization as subjects of physiological investigation, several have had an unexpected result. Out of them a new doctrine of vitalism has arisen, to trouble the even progress of biological thought. Not many years ago such a development would have been considered simply impossible. But in reality there is a more difficult

[1] This concept is developed in *Die organischen Regulationen*, Leipzig, 1901.

riddle hidden in the fact of regulation than at first appears. And gradually, with the transition from the older purely analytical investigation to the modern more synthetic researches, this riddle has been revealed.

The principal figure in the new development is Professor Hans Driesch. His thought originates in the idea, whose foundation we have just traced, that the phenomena of regulation disclose "Teleology as an irreducible peculiarity of the phenomena of life." This standpoint is quite unexceptionable. But while it has led the greater number of investigators merely to redouble their efforts toward a mechanistic description of the various organic regulations, Driesch has sought to utilize such descriptions as a means to overthrow the mechanistic theory itself. In his opinion no machine could possibly produce many of the phenomena of regulation.

It may be at once conceded that nobody has ever given a mechanistic explanation of a single organic regulatory process. In spite of this, however, many simple mechanical analogues like the thermostat and the gyroscope are well known. As an explanation of the present state of the question we may consider the regulation of the temperature of the human body. There exists an admirable description of the various methods by which the tendency to a rise or fall of temperature is counteracted. Conduction, convection, and radiation of heat and the evaporation of water are all involved. These are varied according to the condition of the organism and its environment. The process is controlled in a most intricate manner through the operation of physiological activities such as the distribution of the blood in the different parts of the body and the intervention of the sweat glands. Beneath these conditions in turn is the regulation of the production of heat, which at need rises and falls so as to preserve the equilibrium. Under ordinary circumstances the oxidation of carbohydrate alone may be concerned in this fluctuation, but, if the supply of carbohydrate fails, other substances will be employed in its stead. Moreover, all of these processes are involved in and modified by other physiological activities such as the performance of mechanical work.

Clearly the physiologist is here confronted by an incomplete, but yet partially successful mechanistic account of one element of the functional organization of the human body. But how is the process governed ? By what chain of mechanical causation does a fall in the temperature cause a rise in the rate of oxidation ? This question, in turn, is not altogether beyond the scope of our present physiological investigations. But sooner or later, when the problem is studied, we come upon the fact that a certain organ or group of cells accom-

plishes that which is requisite to the preservation
of the equilibrium, varying the internal conditions
according to the variation of the external conditions, in a manner which we can on no account at
present explain. The same difficulty is encountered
in the analysis of every other organic regulation, of
whatever sort. There is no physiological phenomenon of regulation the *autonomy* of which we can
today understand. This is Haldane's ground for
the rejection of mechanism.

The distinction here involved is by no means
easy to grasp. In the qualitative researches of
experimental morphology, from which Driesch's
speculations arise, the difficulty of understanding
how our knowledge is restricted becomes magnified. But it remains even in the quantitative investigations of physico-chemical regulation. One
thing is evident, we possess no good device for
imagining a cell at work, and until we can do this
we shall never know just what to think about any
regulation. This, at least, is a fact on which mechanists and vitalists can agree.

It may, perhaps, be said that in performing such
functions as adjusting the regulatory processes,
cells seem to act as if they were controlled by
something which remotely resembles intelligence,
but which is really far superior in efficiency, in that
it operates necessarily, according to the needs of
the moment, without the guide of previous expe-

rience, and without those errors of judgment which are all too common in voluntary action. Such is the entelechy of Driesch. Driesch's effort to prove the existence of entelechy in the organism culminates in what he regards as a demonstration that mechanism is necessarily unable to determine some of the phenomena of organic regulation. In the absence of any clear understanding of the operation of cell mechanisms, such an effort is, I think, clearly in vain. It may carry conviction to those who are already predisposed in its favor, but no one else can accept the argument, and an opponent will always regard it as worthless.

The opponents of Driesch are in certain respects better equipped than he is for the controversy, because they are able to appeal to the authority of general principles of science. There is, for instance, the theory of natural selection. That has already had a large share in overwhelming the older vitalistic speculations. For it undertakes to reveal the development of all the most complex forms of life out of the simplest forms, as the result of a purely mechanical process. And whoever accepts it may be disposed to regard the original organism itself as trapped in a stable form, according to that principle of the survival of a dynamic equilibrium which Hume had recognized.[1]

[1] Above, p. 49.

From such a beginning Darwin's evolution might proceed. This appears to be the view of Roux. Hume's idea is, indeed, just as applicable to any other material system as, in a refined form, it has proved to be to the organism. But this criticism of Driesch is not decisive. In the first place it begs the question, for the nature of regulations is at issue in the problem of evolution. Further it is now evident that we are not justified in regarding our existing mechanistic theories as sufficient completely to explain the evolutionary process. And finally, any theory about the origin of life is nothing but an unfounded guess.

But there is a far more formidable objection to vitalism. More explicitly than ever before the modern principles of physical science seem to compel us to recognize absolute mechanical necessity in all things. We may not understand organic regulations, or organic evolution, or the origin of life; in fact we are still unable with the necessary clearness to represent to ourselves the structure of a cell; yet these are at least phenomena. As phenomena they are subject to the laws governing all phenomena, that is to say to the two laws of thermodynamics. For the laws of conservation and degradation of energy have long since supplanted Leibniz's rudimentary idea of the conservation of *vis viva*, as the ground of our conception of necessary causation.

Now the laws of thermodynamics contemplate all forms of activity, not merely mechanical force, but heat, light, electricity, and the rest, in all kinds of material systems, not merely among moving masses, but in gases, electrical machines, steam engines, and all others. We have a good deal of experimental evidence that they hold for the living organism. And everywhere they are believed to involve that same absolutely necessary mechanical determination which Leibniz had postulated upon a more slender foundation.

It is important to understand the foundation of the belief in mechanical determination, which seems to be as follows: The world of physical science consists of matter and energy existing in space and time; in any particular case these four things are always to be represented by mathematical terms which are functionally related together in the equations expressing the laws of physical science. This functional relationship, although often unknown, is believed to be rigorously and unequivocally determined by the laws. Therefore, in accordance with the laws of conservation and the second law of thermodynamics, the non-mechanical, i. e. any factor which is non-material, non-energetic, non-spatial, and non-temporal, cannot enter into or modify any physical or chemical process. Thus "vital" processes can no more modify mechanical determination than mechanical processes can modify geometrical determination, and mechanism is conceived to be no less absolutely a condition of life than geometry of mechanics.

Driesch is not unmindful of this difficulty. As a way out he suggests that entelechy may, perhaps, operate by suspending, as occasion requires, the operation of the second law of thermodynamics. This theory is ingenious, but I believe untenable. In fact it involves a reduction to the sphere of molecules of the old fallacy of Descartes. For to suspend the operation of the second law of thermodynamics would be precisely equivalent to an alteration, without the expenditure of energy, of the direction of motion of the particles of a material body. Under these conditions an object which had fallen to the ground might, by cooling itself, rise again into the air. Nothing could be more radically inconsistent with the fundamental principles of physical science, as now generally admitted, than this assumption or the theory which it is designed to support.

Driesch's discussions also extend to voluntary action, which is the most familiar means to the foundation of vitalistic theories. But, except in one important respect, the ground for a conclusion favorable to the vitalistic hypothesis is here identical with that in the case of the organic regulation. The difference consists in the fact that we know the mind, but not the entelechy. In fact everybody is conscious of his ability at will to change the course of mechanical events in the world around him. No conviction of the truth of the principles of physical science, however firmly grounded in scientific and philosophical criticism, can ever eradicate this belief. As a practical guide in daily life it is perfectly indispensable. Yet there seems to be a conflict between the belief and the principles of thermodynamics.

It is a strange irony that the principles of science should seem to deny the necessary conviction of common sense. For was it not a similar denial of the external world that led men of science to their most contemptuous rejection of metaphysics? And if Berkeley's idealism is to be rejected in so far as it denies the real existence of our tables and chairs, then the principles of thermodynamics must be rejected in so far as they deny the justice of our common-sense idea of voluntary action.

But another kind of consideration further complicates this problem, for the common-sense notion of voluntary action is badly in need of analysis. The most elementary of psychological considerations leads us to the perception that our choice of action, even though it be conceived as the result of no mechanical process, is yet far from free. Not only does our whole past experience provide us with the material for choice, but it rigorously limits the choice. In spite of ourselves we do always act in

character, and the suspicion cannot be escaped
that all mental processes may be unequivocally
determined. If this be admitted we have once
more arrived at the conception of a world in which
all is in some sense absolute necessity.

Yet even then the psycho-physical riddle persists. In truth it is undiminished, for how does the
psychical determination get its effect in the physical world ? How does an idea change the course of
events ? Is the relationship a mere illusion ? Is
there merely a pre-established harmony between
the two absolutely independent worlds of mind
and matter ? That common sense cannot tolerate
such a view is proved by the experience of more
than two centuries. But physical science seems to
deny the possibility of any other theory, unless we
admit that mind is a mere epiphenomenon upon a
mechanical process in the nervous system. The
latter process would then become a part of the
chain of physical causation and the difficulty
would be removed from physical science. But
what becomes of the biological function of consciousness, upon this assumption ? Consciousness
was never produced in the process of evolution
merely as an impotent accompaniment of reflex
action. Obviously there is a necessary postulate
of biology which declares that in its simplest form
the function of consciousness is a regulation of the
reflex processes in such a way as to modify in a

peculiar manner the chain of mechanical causation. The question is to discover how, if at all, this can be itself a mechanistic process. The vitalistic reply is that a mechanistic explanation of the phenomena of the most trivial voluntary action is impossible.

Driesch's view of this argument in favor of vitalism is as follows: " Any real action is an *individual* answer to an individual stimulus — founded upon the historical basis.

" And this individual correspondence, occurring upon an historically created basis, cannot be understood as a case of mechanical causality. For there is not a ' sum ' on the side of the stimulus that corresponds to a ' sum ' on the side of the reaction, and, further, not even the possibilities of acting are in any way ' preformed.'

" From this point of view, the brain and the nervous system appear as nothing but a necessary means for putting the ' acting ' factor in connexion with material nature, but they are not themselves the acting factor." [1]

This result appears to be substantially identical with the conclusion of Hobhouse's careful analysis of the same problem:

" In a simple purposive action — where I require a book which I remember to have left in a particular place and go to fetch it, my memory, which, mechanically interpreted, must be some

---

[1] *The History and Theory of Vitalism*, London, 1914, p. 213.

deposit of the effect of my previous dealing with
the book in my brain, is so combined with my need
and my physical surroundings as to discharge in
succession the actions appropriate to fetching the
book. This deposit — complex enough in that it
must have its exact point to point correspondences
with the several physical relations of the rooms of
the house, etc. — is only one among the millions of
deposits that my experience has formed. Yet
provision must be made for selecting it out of
them, and bringing it, and none other, to bear upon
the physical tension, which may be supposed to
correspond to my felt need, and thereby to effect
the successive discharge of a complex series of
actions. If we try to formulate a general plan for
effecting such selection and correlation, we find
ourselves speaking of a state of want, picking out
from experience whatever is relevant to its satis-
faction, and guiding action accordingly. But
though we might find terms other than these which
would avoid all reference to feeling or consciousness, the explanation would imply that there exists
a something determined in its actions by their relation to their results, i. e. something purposive.
Abstract the notion of the relevancy of the means
to end, and the bottom of the whole proceeding
tumbles out. In short, in the activity which we
claim as purposive, we find repeatedly that one
factor of our life (e. g. an experience) may be

brought to bear upon another (e. g. a want) in a manner that varies indefinitely from case to case. The only principle uniting the otherwise unique combinations is that of the relevance of the combination to the end. Admit this principle, and we recognize a structure determined by purpose. Deny it, and we have no general plan to explain the unique combinations. Either horn of the dilemma excludes mechanism.

" The denial of purposive causation, therefore, is not suggested but repelled by general experience, and owes its existence only to the theory that everything must act by mechanical laws. But this theory is a pure assumption, which derives its apparent cogency from confusion with the quite different principle that everything must act in accordance with some law. The leading mechanical principles I take to be adequately proved for mechanism, and, therefore, for any structure which is purely mechanical. Now the organism is a physical structure, but to assume that all its actions conform to mechanical laws is to assume that it is a physical structure only. Consciousness directly informs us that it is more than this — that it is . . . a psycho-physical whole." [1]

At this point I cannot help thinking that Hobhouse has momentarily lost his grip on the argu-

[1] Hobhouse, *Development and Purpose.* London, 1913, pp. 325, 326.

ment. Consciousness does indeed inform us that the organism is more than a physical structure; no doubt it is a psycho-physical whole. Accordingly some of its actions do not, strictly speaking, conform to mechanical laws.[1] An instance of this is choice or any other psychical activity. But, even so, it involves a further assumption to assert that the *physical* activities of the organism even when parts of psycho-physical activities can ever be explained as not in conformity with mechanical laws.[2] Countless attempts so to represent them have been made and they have all failed.

What Hobhouse seems to mean is that, if we are to understand the true nature of organic activity, we must not consider the physical structure at all. In short we must adopt Haldane's view that the concept of organization somehow excludes or eliminates that of mechanism and is inconsistent with it. This seems to be implied in a later statement:

" In this account the living being is regarded as a system of what must be called forces, in which mechanical relations are qualified by teleological relations. When these two sets of relations are hypostatised as Mind and Body they become two substances, and in place of a system whose mode of action as a whole departs from that of mechanical systems in virtue of its specific quality, we have

[1] But see below, p. 113.

[2] Cf. the relation of geometry to mechanics: mechanics is more than geometry, but never ungeometrical.

the problem of interaction between two distinct and separate systems, each with laws of its own. If interaction is admitted, we have the conception of body as a purely mechanical system, whose operations at a certain point come plumply to an end, while at another point they as plumply begin, the intervening stage being filled by actions within the other system. Body is thus a purely mechanical system which does not conform to laws which, it is not denied, are adequately proved for mechanical systems. To escape this conclusion it must be admitted that Mind exerts force and is acted on by force. But Mind was precisely the concentrated essence of that which is opposed to force. Thus the contradiction of a purely mechanical system which does not act mechanically is balanced by the contradiction of a non-mechanical system which does act mechanically. To escape from this dilemma the Parallelistic scheme is propounded, according to which the mental and the bodily run on side by side in point to point correspondence, but without interaction. This scheme, however, in effect renders the mental element superfluous. A complication of mechanism is all that is required to explain the actions of living beings. On the other hand, the rise of the psychical stream in coincidence with a certain point of the physical, and its disappearance at another point, are left unexplained." [1]

[1] Hobhouse, *Development and Purpose*, p. 329, note.

So far as I can understand the problem, Hobhouse's arguments and those of Driesch before him against the mechanistic character of the mental processes involved in voluntary action are at present unanswerable. But, in view of our present ignorance of the underlying phenomena, they may fairly be regarded as inconclusive. On this subject we simply do not know what we are talking about. No doubt these processes have their physical basis, but the fact remains that science, like philosophy, cannot regard thoughts as the activities of material systems. All attempts that have been made in this direction are unworthy of the slightest consideration. Nevertheless biology is obliged to assert that ideas, whatever the philosopher may think of them, *at least* have a function, and that function, physiologically considered, can only be to regulate action. Thus we come to the conclusion that ideas, which are nevertheless non-material and non-mechanical, do change the course of mechanical processes. We may hope that in time this difficulty will somehow be circumvented. Meanwhile I think it is true that Hobhouse's own resolution of the difficulty, like that of Lotze or of Leibniz, is unacceptable to science.

If this be so we are confronted by a genuine paradox. Looking at physico-chemical phenomena on the one hand, we declare that the principles of thermodynamics fully prove absolute mechanical determinism in all material systems of whatever nature. Turning then to the phenomena of voluntary action, we can see no escape from the view that, if determinism be universal, it is not at least always in the strict sense mechanical. The only principle of determination in the sequence of events seems to be teleological. Who indeed can so far forget common sense as to deny this in the case of any plan ? Here is a stark contradiction.

This psycho-physical paradox is one of the most tormenting that the human mind has ever constructed, and countless efforts have been made to escape from it. One of the most curious of these is the *tychism* of Charles Peirce. According to this idea the laws of nature possess not an absolute but only a statistical character.[1] Not even the laws of conservation are absolutely true, but they are only approximations. In this approximate character there is found the possibility of a belief that the psychical may impinge upon the physical; that mind may move matter. A somewhat similar theory, but more in accord with the ideas of most men of science, has been propounded by the eminent mathematical physicist, Boussinesq.[2] This is developed from the theory of singular integrals in differential equations. And the conclusion is

---

[1] This, of course, is Maxwell's view of the second law of thermodynamics.

[2] *Conciliation du véritable détermination mécanique avec l'existence de la vie et de la liberté morale.* Paris, 1878.

reached that mechanical processes are conceivable which arrive at situations where a further progress in one or another direction might be determined without the expenditure of energy. Thus the mind, even though it has no energy to expend, might determine the outcome of such a process.

This idea may be regarded as a further development from the theory of Descartes on the basis of Leibniz's criticism. The principal conclusion is thus stated: " The equations of motion of the organ of thought admit of singular integrals; and for geometry these integrals are the expression of the influence of morals upon physics. In this mysterious field two coexistent orders which are perceived as quite distinct — on the one hand the geometrical or material order extended in space, on the other the psychological or moral order comprising that rich web of sentiments, thoughts, and volitions whose interconnections and successions constitute the marvelous spectacle of our inner life — correspond and touch each other. It is in this field, the only one where it may set foot without ceasing to be free, that the mind, deprived of all material force, succeeds in ruling the world of material things. Here it directs and conquers the blind forces which struggle for dominion, by setting them against one another. Here it modifies the geometrical order of objects, without being obliged to find in their actual state the principle of its determinations, but rather guiding itself by a prevision of a future which exists only for the mind, and realizing plans ideally conceived in view of a desired end." [1]

This theory rests upon a mathematical formulation of that view of contingency which from Cournot to M. Boutroux has been so prominent a feature of French philosophical thought. There can be no doubt, if the mathematical analysis is sound, if singular integrals are indeed possible for the unknown differential equations which mathematically express any of the phenomena of the central nervous system, that a possible escape from the psycho-physical difficulty becomes conceivable.

But it must be remarked that the peculiarities of an equation cannot help us to imagine mind operating upon matter. And it may be asked if the theory does not prove too much. Is it not destructive, ideally regarded, of all mechanical determinations? These, however, are not questions which now concern us, for they are not involved in the history of the teleological problem. The ideas of Boussinesq, like those of Peirce, have not yet exerted an appreciable influence upon thought. It

[1] Boussinesq, *op. cit.*, p. 60. See also for two less consistent theories Cournot, *Traité de l'enchaînement des idées fondamentales dans les sciences et dans l'histoire*, Paris, 1861, i, ch. 4, and Saint-Venant, *Comptes Rendus*, lxxxiv, 419. In the work of Cournot there may be also found an excellent statement of the concept of organization.

is even hardly possible to guess whether the neglect of them may be due to some radical defect which makes them incompatible with scientific thought, or whether they may have fallen into oblivion because those whom they should have interested were unable to understand them.[1]

Thus we come back to two counter propositions, which were rejected by Kant because contradictory, as an expression of the conclusion of two lines of scientific thought in the nineteenth century.

" All production of material things is possible according to merely mechanical laws."

" Some production of material things is not possible according to merely mechanical laws." [2]

These propositions are, indeed, contradictory. But I think there can be no hope of an immediate generally acceptable decision between the two. It is well established that a study of physical science nearly always leads to the first, and that few men can escape the second when, like the historian, they study human actions. At present there seems to be no way open to science of further investigating the question. Conceivably the ideas of Boussinesq and Peirce, foreign as they are to orthodox scienti-

[1] Clerk Maxwell, whose qualifications for the task were the very highest, has discussed this question of freedom in a little essay which may be found in the Appendix. It is to be observed that, though he reaches no conclusion, his discussion revolves about the concepts of singularity and statistics.

[2] *Kritik of Judgment*, pp. 294, 295.

fic thought, may some day lead to a novel development, and of course no one can foresee the new thought of the future. But the counsel of discretion is to leave the question as it stands, and to turn to other matters.

This is the more suitable since, as we have seen, the study of psycho-physical phenomena leads, not to indeterminism, but to a new determinism in which voluntary action is thought to be no less subject to law than inorganic phenomena themselves. Whatever our metaphysical views, this we are obliged to admit as a necessary postulate of scientific research. For we can on no account think about the phenomena except on the assumption that even the most casual of human actions would again necessarily recur if *all* the conditions which preceded it could be perfectly reëstablished. The mind simply cannot escape the necessity of operating in this manner. Even supporters of free intervention admit so much.[1] I shall not however, seek systematically to establish the proposition. It will suffice to note that the whole tendency of psychology is in this direction and that it is generally allowed by the vitalists. Moreover, I think it is evident that the operations of Driesch's entelechies no less than the laws of gravitation would suffer from purely chance occurrences, and this seems to be their author's own view.

[1] Ward, *The Realm of Ends*, Cambridge, 1911, chap. xiv.

The question which remains is, therefore, the old problem of the teleology of nature as a whole. Each advance of the scientific description, Newton's *Principia*, Carnot's *Reflections*, *The Origin of Species*, or the concept of organization, refers some aspect of things as they are to the earliest conceivable state of the universe.

Certain things still seem to have originated quite inexplicably during the course of evolution. Such are life and consciousness, to say nothing of historical events. But the whole tendency of science is either to destroy the novel character of the products of nature by discovering how they did really originate through necessary processes, or else to regard them as contemporaneous and coexistent with the universe itself. We cannot doubt that this process will continue. It is not restricted by the doubts which we have just reviewed, and it does not directly touch certain ethical and philosophical problems which cannot be avoided in the vitalistic controversy. It does not depend upon any particular way of looking at natural phenomena. For it is nothing more than an expression of that general principle of continuity, which from Galileo's discovery of inertia till today has governed all scientific thought. In the course of this movement of thought Driesch's "dynamic" teleology of vitalism loses itself in the larger problem of the " static " teleology of nature, and Bergson's *élan vital,* if it be admitted, becomes a question of detail. I cannot think this altogether a misfortune, for as Professor Bosanquet says: " Purpose only means, *prima facie,* that, using consciousness in the widest sense, some creature consciously wants something. But . . . does the something lose its value when it is attained ? " . . . " Things are not teleological because they are purposed but are purposed because they are teleological." [1]

[1] *The Principle of Individuality and Value.* London, 1912, pp. 136, 137.

VI

NATURE

INFINITELY curious and varied is man's attitude toward nature. The savage, the craftsman, the sailor, the artist, the philosopher and the scientist each contributes to it; yet all seem to advance toward a common understanding. There is no such agreement upon any other great subject in the whole domain of thought, in all the manifold forms of human expression. Cournot has composed a rhapsody upon this theme: " Men early felt the need of a term to designate that hidden power which maintains the cycle of life; to represent it in possession of those attributes which vital phenomena reveal to us, but without a mingling of other ideas suggested by phenomena of another order, such as consciousness of our moral personality, of our reasoned conclusions, of a moral law which governs them, of good and evil. The term which they employ for this purpose is nature taken actively (*Natura naturans*, as the schoolmen had it): an indispensable term, which corresponds to an idea so well determined, yet so hard to define, that we see all the world making use of it, the believer and the skeptic, the philosophers of all sects and the learned of all schools, those who profess the

grossest materialism and those who enshroud
themselves in the cloudiest mysticism alike. There
must indeed be a reason for such an agreement, and
this reason is the need of distinguishing and marking off that which equally impresses every one, that
which every one feels obliged to recognize, to
whatever philosophical or religious system his
reason or his faith may attach him. It is as if
there were a territory whose neutralization had
been prescribed by a common interest, in order to
carry elsewhere the ardors of war. Whether we
believe in a supernatural providence which in its
goodness and justice rewards and punishes, which
yields to prayers and repentance, or reject this
consolatory dogma, still must we admit that in the
visible world, save for humanity, the action of the
supreme cause only manifests itself deprived of
such moral attributes, as it suffices for a world
where morality has no place.

" The idea of nature is the idea of inexpressible
divine power and divine art, beyond comparison or
measure with man's powers and industry, impress-
ing on its works an intrinsic character of majesty
and grace, yet operating under the sway of necessary conditions, tending fatally and inexorably to
an end which surpasses us, yet in such manner that
the mysterious chain of finality, whose origin and
term we cannot scientifically demonstrate, appears
to us as a guiding thread, with whose help order

introduces itself into the observed facts, and we find the trace of the subject of our investigations." [1]

Is it indeed vain to seek an explanation of the order of nature beyond the laws of nature's uniformity ? So it would appear to one who regards but the surface of things. Only the poetic philosopher like Cournot or the philosophical poet like Goethe seems to find something more. Yet positive thought can never rest in the face of such a question, and I think that it has found a clue. But if we are to grasp this clue we must ascend to a region of colder thought.

Lachelier is one of the most notable successors of Cournot in France. He is known for his brief essay on induction, but has produced little beside to indicate the originality of his mind. His essay consists in a metaphysical examination of the problem why nature is such that the inductive process lays bare our scientific laws. And he reaches a novel conclusion.

In his opinion the fundamental axiom of induction is that in living beings as in all material objects the conditions of the existence of phenomena are absolutely determined. Accepting this view it is easy to see how we can pass from the fact to the law. For the conditions of any case must then be identical with those of every case of a phenomenon.

[1] *Traité de l'enchaînement des idées fondamentales dans les sciences et dans l'histoire*, Paris, 1861, vol. 1, pp. 497, 498.

But this is not all, for in addition to the laws which we thus recognize there is also the law of organization. And, as Lachelier believes, a similar principle of order is to be seen in the inorganic world. " The conception of laws of nature seems, therefore, to be founded on two distinct principles: one by virtue of which phenomena constitute series, in which the existence of the preceding determines that of the succeeding; the other by virtue of which these series in turn constitute systems in which the idea of the whole determines the existence of the parts." (In Lachelier's opinion this is especially to be seen in chemistry.) " In a word, we may say that the possibility of induction depends on the double principle of efficient causes and final causes." [1]

This idea is also stated on the ground of a discrimination between the existence of serial unity or causal enchainment and unity of system or harmonious unity in nature.[2] If I rightly understand the idea, Kepler's first and second laws, considered with regard to one planet alone, would be an illustration of serial unity, Kepler's third law might be, and the periodic classification of the elements certainly would be an illustration of systematic unity.

[1] Lachelier, *Du fondement de l'induction*, Paris, 1871, p. 16.
[2] *Ibid.*, p. 83.

Again the idea is put forward as follows: " While the mechanism of nature fills up, by a continuous evolution, the infinity of time and space, the finality of this same nature, on the contrary, concentrates itself in a multitude of systems, which are indeed distinct, but yet analogous to one another."[1] But, moreover, every phenomenon is in fact mechanically determined, not merely by those phenomena which precede it in time but also, as Lachelier points out, by all those which accompany it in space.

Without following Lachelier in his more strictly metaphysical discussions, we may note a final observation, that, if finality is in all phenomena the hidden spring of mechanism, there is nothing in the formation of an organism which exceeds the ordinary powers of nature, and which requires the interference of a special principle.[2]

The essential idea of Lachelier's essay seems to be that the chains of causation in nature weave themselves into an intelligible pattern, and that this pattern, quite as much as the chains of causation, is the subject of our scientific investigations. Through this, as Cournot has said, " We find the trace of the subjects of our investigations."

Now there can be no doubt that this is true, at least in part. For Hume's idea of the survival of

---

[1] *Loc. cit.*, p. 90.
[2] Cf. *The Fitness of the Environment*, p. 300.

dynamic equilibria is but an example of such a process, and it meets all the conditions of Lachelier's analysis.

The ideas of this essay on induction are somewhat similar to the central points in Lotze's philosophical system. They appear to be even closer to certain opinions now held by Professor Bosanquet.[1] The English metaphysician is concerned to reveal the error of those who "rest the case of teleology within the universe exclusively on the capacity of finite consciousness for guidance and selection." [2] This of course, though contemplating mere psycho-physical action, is to found a discussion exclusively on the logic of the extreme vitalistic position. In Bosanquet's opinion such a philosophy "is going near to destroy the idea of the reign of law, and to enthrone the finite subject as the guide and master of nature and history." [3] But "it is vain to look to the bare fact of conscious purpose for the essence or significance of teleology." [4] In truth not conscious purpose but universal determination is essential to the existence of a plan in nature. For "plan involves determinateness, and determinateness continuity, and that in all directions. Everything must be followed by something — must be continued by something on

[1] "The Meaning of Teleology," *Proceedings of the British Academy*, ii, p. 235.   April 30, 1906.

[2] *Ibid.*, p. 235.   [3] *Ibid.*, p. 235.   [4] *Ibid.*, p. 236.

every side, and between any two somethings
within a unity there must be a determinate inter-
connexion, prescribed by the content of that
unity." [1] "Mind and individuality, so far as
finite, find their fullest expression as aspects of very
complex and precisely determined mechanical
systems. This is the law, I believe wholly without
exception, for every higher product of human soul
and intelligence, and also of cosmic evolution. The
mechanical appearance must be granted to be universal and unbroken." [2] Yet from this point of
view " we can freely suppose the world-plan to be
immanent in the whole, including finite mind and
also mechanical nature." [3] " It is impossible . . .
to treat part of the world as primary and part as a
secondary superstructure. We must interpret the
nature of nature as much by the flower as by the
law of gravitation. If we come to that, there are
appearances, which we cannot on any sound principle refuse to call teleological, in the most direct
and simple reactions of mechanism." [4] " . . . the
foundations of teleology in the universe are far too
deeply laid to be accounted for by, still less restricted to, the intervention of finite consciousness.

[1] *Loc. cit.*, p. 238.

[2] *Ibid.*, p. 240. This is of course not meant as an assertion that
the operations of mind are to be regarded as physico-chemical processes, indeed the term mechanical is here used in rather too general a
sense for the purpose of scientific analysis.

[3] *Ibid.*, p. 240.   [4] *Ibid.*, p. 241.

Everything goes to show that such consciousness should not be regarded as the source of teleology, but as itself a manifestation, falling within wider manifestations, of the immanent individuality of the real." [1]

" The contrast, then, of mechanism with teleology, is not to be treated as if elucidated at one blow by the antithesis of purposive consciousness, and the reactions of part on part. It is rooted in the very nature of totality, which it regards from two complementary points of view, as an individual whole, and as constituted of interreacting members. Of the two points of view, it is impossible for either to be entirely absent. Assuming this impossibility to be possible, a total failure of mechanical intelligibility would reduce the spiritual to the miraculous, and destroy teleology, as a total failure of teleological intelligibility would reduce individuality to incoherence, and annihilate mechanism." [2]

As philosophical doctrine of the present day I can see no escape from Bosanquet's conclusions. At the very least it is a necessary postulate of science " that the mechanical [i. e., naturally determined] appearance must be granted to be universal and unbroken." However interesting may be the organism as such, however alluring the vitalist's conception of the world, these, without determin-

---

[1] *Loc. cit.*, p. 242.   [2] *Ibid.*, p. 244.

ism, are no secure foundation for a philosophy. Rather are they greatly involved in the rapid movement of scientific thought. There is indeed in the *concept* of organization that which has defied time and change, and endured from Aristotle to our own day. But the organism is now under investigation. Year by year we see more clearly, in accordance with elementary physical concepts and quantitative measurements, what is the nature of this harmonious unity.

The advance of science has assuredly not made the origin of life easier to imagine, or even to think about. On the contrary I am fully persuaded that it has made the task far more difficult. Least of all does it lead us unduly to prize those analogies between organic and inorganic phenomena that have been so much discussed. The growth of a crystal and of a living body are less similar than the growth of a bank account and of a great commercial " organization." The dynamic equilibria of life and of a whirl-pool are entirely unequal in complexity and in the very essence of the physical and chemical processes by which they are adjusted and controlled.

Yet it is quite impossible to escape from the idea of living things as natural products, for science involves determinism and determinism imposes this very concept. With the increase of our knowledge of organization we see ever more clearly the interdependence of all living things and the harmony between the organism and its environment. This leads us to a conception of the organism as intrinsically a part of nature and so to the idea of nature as a whole. The essential feature of Cournot's position regarding the necessity of thus hypostatizing nature is today better than ever before justified by science. And thus the problem of the teleological form and behavior of the organism merges in the larger question of the order of nature. Nothing can oppose the tendency toward this idea; it is the modern echo of Aristotle's thought, which made him seek " the character of the material nature whose necessary results have been made available by rational nature for a final cause." [1]

Thus we arrive at a clear philosophical conclusion. But science can never accept this result until it has been founded upon the scientific evidence by a process of scientific reasoning. And it is only too apparent that progress in this direction has been scarcely perceptible. We do indeed scientifically recognize the truth of Hume's concept of the tendency of dynamic equilibria to survive. The living thing itself is one example and Newton's *Principia* gives a full account of another. But though Newton himself and many others have not failed to form teleological inferences from such

[1] Above, p. 17.

facts, these have never been generally accepted
as scientifically valid. However teleological may
be the appearance of the products of nature, the
teleology of nature itself cannot be scientifically
established unless some kind of connection, conceivable only as teleological, can be shown to exist
among nature's laws.

Lachelier has imagined such a relation and employed it as the foundation of his philosophical
thought. But it is very doubtful if science can ever
thoroughly establish such a proposition. The
exhaustive examination of all the laws of nature
from this or any other point of view is quite inconceivable, if for no other reason, because we shall
never know them all. And perhaps science can
never decide whether the organic and the inorganic
are ultimately to be philosophically conceived as a
single order, for the task of scientific synthesis will
never be completed.

Nevertheless we may now see that the whole
movement of scientific and philosophical thought
upon this subject does lead to a more modest scientific problem. For if it be quite inconceivable that
science should ever completely solve the riddle of
the order of nature, it is clear that nothing but the
inherent difficulty of scientific research is to hinder
an inquiry, step by step, into the problem. In
biology this question has long been recognized and
efforts to understand the origin of life, as well as to

account for the process of organic evolution, have followed. But at this point of attack the difficulties are almost insurmountable. Therefore, in spite of Darwin's great labors, we remain largely in ignorance. Apart from the imperfect generalization of natural selection and the rudimentary beginnings of a science of heredity, we still have but the vaguest ideas concerning the development of living things as products of nature. And regarding their origin we have no ideas at all.

The simpler and more general problem of the teleology of nature as a whole has been neither recognized nor investigated by science. Yet the problem is now clear enough. All men admit in the teleological appearance of the world something that is real. There is order, stability, and a richly varied collocation of material objects at the basis of it. When we think of the solar system, the meteorological cycle and the organic cycle we distinguish that which quite inevitably and directly impresses us as harmonious. Now, as we have seen, it is no longer permissible to doubt that this impression of harmony corresponds to an order in the universe. No doubt science must put aside the philosophical problems which thus arise, and philosophy must deny to all men the right to found a system of natural theology upon the fact. But it is a false and discredited metaphysical hypothesis which leads to the denial of the order of nature as a subject of scientific research. How then is the production of this order to be scientifically explained ? What is the mechanistic origin of the present order of nature ?

Only if we turn to the facts concerning the evolution of our solar system and of the earth can we investigate the problem. But in following this as a special case of the whole cosmic process we are in danger of bewilderment. The natural history of the earth involves a mass of particular facts which are not yet well coördinated and can seldom be referred to the laws which govern them.

If, however, we seek a more general and abstract point of view, we find a clearer issue. This process of the evolution of our world, however manifold in its details, is at least governed and directed by the general laws of physical science. It cannot be doubted that others among them beside the tendency to formation and survival of stable systems, as formulated by Newton for dynamics, by Darwin for biology, and by Le Chatelier for physical chemistry, are intelligibly concerned in the production of the order of nature. In like manner the properties of matter and energy are concerned. It is clear, therefore, that the real scientific problem may be approximately solved by discovering, step by step, how the general laws of physical science work together upon the properties of matter and energy so as to produce that order. Thus, and thus only, can we understand it. Speculation *a priori* on such a question is in vain; only the scientific investigation can reach a result; only this scientific result can determine the importance of the question for philosophy.

Somewhat vaguely, from the biological point of view, I have already discussed one aspect of this problem.[1] In the following pages the question will be investigated more rigorously and systematically according to the principles of physical science.

[1] *The Fitness of the Environment*, New York, 1913. " The Functions of an Environment," *Science*, N.S., xxxix, p. 524.

VII

EVOLUTION

In the history of thought there is, beside the establishment of the second law of thermodynamics, one systematic effort to discover a general law of nature governing the whole process of evolution. This is to be found in Herbert Spencer's *First Principles*, where it serves as the foundation for his Synthetic Philosophy. This law of evolution, as its author called it, is developed from a rather vague conception not unlike Lachelier's later ideas. Spencer perceived that we can know a complex phenomenon only when we understand both its elements and how these elements coöperate in order to produce it. " That which alone can unify knowledge must be the law of coöperation of all the factors — a law expressing simultaneously the complex antecedents and the complex consequents which any phenomenon as a whole presents." [1] Such a law, Spencer declares, must be regarded as quite generally valid, for: " If the law of operation of each factor holds true throughout the cosmos, so, too, must the law of their coöperation." [2]

---

[1] *First Principles*, New York, reprinted from the fifth London edition, p. 468.　　[2] *Ibid.*, p. 468.

In Spencer's opinion this law is apparent in all the phenomena of evolution; it governs all production and dissipation, and necessarily concerns matter and motion alike. Such is " the law of the entire cycle of changes passed through by every existence — loss of motion and consequent integration, eventually followed by gain of motion and consequent disintegration. Besides applying to the whole history of each existence, it applies to each detail of the history. Both processes are going on at every instant; but always there is a differential result in favor of the first or the second. And every change, even though it be only a transposition of parts, inevitably advances the one process or the other." [1] " There is habitually a passage from homogeneity to heterogeneity along with the passage from diffusion to concentration. While the matter composing the solar system has been assuming a denser form, it has changed from unity to variety of distribution. Solidification of the earth has been accompanied by a progress from comparative uniformity to extreme multiformity. In the course of its advance from a germ to a mass of relatively great bulk, every plant and animal also advances from simplicity to complexity. The increase of a society in numbers and consolidation has for its concomitant an increased heterogeneity both of its political and its industrial organization.

[1] *Loc. cit.*, p. 469.

And the like holds of all super-organic products —
language, science, art and literature." [1]

" In all evolutions, inorganic, organic and super-
organic, this change in the arrangement of matter
is accompanied by a parallel change in the arrangement of motion; every increase in structural
complexity involving a corresponding increase in
functional complexity." [2]

All this depends, in the first place, upon the
fact that " Any finite homogeneous aggregate
must inevitably lose its homogeneity, through
the unequal exposure of its parts to incident
forces." [3]   In Spencer's opinion this instability of
the homogeneous is a perfectly universal phenomenon; it holds for the parts as well as for the
complete system. As a result there is a progressive
tendency for the less heterogeneous to become more
heterogeneous. This tendency even advances,
according to his quaintly simple mathematical
view, in a geometrical progression as the effects
multiply.

Such a process can end only in equilibrium.
" That continual division and subdivision of
forces which changes the uniform into the multiform and the multiform into the more multiform,
is a process by which forces are perpetually dissi-
pated, and dissipation of them continuing as long

[1] *Loc. cit.*, p. 471.   [3] *Ibid.*, p. 473.
[2] *Ibid.*, p. 471.

as there remain any forces unbalanced by opposing forces must end in rest." [1]

" This general principle of equilibration . . . was traced throughout all forms of evolution — astronomic, geologic, biologic, mental and social. And our concluding inference was that the penultimate stage of equilibration, in which the extremest multiformity and most complex moving equilibrium are established, must be one implying the highest conceivable state of humanity." [2]

From this exposition it is apparent that, whatever philosophical use he may have made of it, Spencer believed his *law of evolution* to be a well-founded induction, and, therefore, a law of nature. In this he was probably mistaken. There is indeed a measure of truth in the so-called " law." And his generalizations, regarded as provisional and tentative hypotheses, possess genuine importance. But Spencer seems to have had no idea how arduous would be the task of establishing such a principle even in physical science. He had literally no conception of the nature of the problem which he was raising, for rigorous mathematical proof was foreign to his nature. Under the circumstances it is not surprising to find his views meeting the open hostility of mathematical physicists like Lord Kelvin, Clerk Maxwell, and Tait.[3]

---

[1] *Loc. cit.*, p. 475.   [2] *Ibid.*, p. 475.
[3] Cf. Knott's *Life of Tait*, pp. 281–288, Cambridge, 1911.

At this very time, however, Willard Gi.. attacking the problem of heterogeneous equiliu rium in a rigorous manner, with a full mathematical equipment, a clear understanding of the principles of thermodynamics, and a power in the formation of abstract concepts hardly rivaled in our time. Maxwell at once perceived the connection with Spencer's theories, and wrote to Tait: " Have you (read) Willard Gibbs on Equilibrium of Heterogeneous Substances ? Refreshing after H. Spencer on the Instability of the Homogeneous." [1] This investigation indeed leads to that very " blank form of a universe " which, according to Tait,[2] is the outcome of Spencer's speculation.

One great result of Willard Gibbs's thermodynamic researches was to establish the concept of a *system* as a genuine abstraction. Until the results of his labors were published the mathematical physicists possessed rigorous definitions of time, space, and mass. These, with the aid of their various quantitative measurements, enabled them, after the example of dynamics, to treat many problems quite rigorously and exhaustively. But, wherever chemical composition or constitution was involved they were powerless. If we may judge by the published works on this subject, even Newton had contented himself with the demonstration that mass is independent of chemical composition.

[1] *Loc. cit.*, p. 284.   [2] *Nature*, November 25, 1880.

The significance of the new ideas is readily apparent. Thus the concept of a line is a pure abstraction, for geometrical lines do not exist in nature. Nevertheless it is necessary for the very existence of geometry. The concept of mass, independent of all other forces than gravitation, is a similar fiction; for electrical, magnetic, and other forces, are never quite absent; but it is indispensable to the development of dynamics. In like manner the concept of an *independent system* is a pure creation of the imagination. For no material system is or can ever be perfectly isolated from the rest of the world. Nevertheless it completes the mathematician's "blank form of a universe" without which his investigations are impossible. It enables him to introduce into his geometrical space, not only masses and configurations, but also physical structure and chemical composition. Just as Newton first conclusively showed that this is a world of masses, so Willard Gibbs first revealed it as a world of systems.

In this way physical chemistry has learned what manner of world is the subject of its investigations. It is a world made up of systems and nothing else. This conception of the universe, like that of classical dynamics, which perceives only masses, is both exhaustive and rigorous, though purely imaginary and abstract. It is true that the gravest practical difficulties are sometimes involved, and that these difficulties have led to certain widespread misconceptions. Thus, the modern chemist hardly realizes the necessity of taking account of electrical and various other forces in his definition of systems. Yet such forces are much more generally involved in the phenomena of heterogeneous equilibrium than in those with which dynamics is concerned, and they were discussed in Gibbs's original publication. But such fallacies regard practice and not the principle itself.

The characteristics of a system are revealed in Gibbs's development of his mathematical analysis. They do not appear as entirely novel concepts, but like those of line and mass, as the results of old familiar ideas transformed by critical analysis. The proximate subordinate parts of a system or isolated aggregate of matter are the phases. A phase is, first of all, a homogeneous body. " We may call such bodies as differ in composition or state different *phases* of the matter concerned, regarding all bodies which differ only in quantity and form as different examples of the same phase."[1] Accordingly a phase may be solid, liquid, or gaseous. Its only essential characteristic as such is physical and chemical homogeneity within the limits of our analysis. It is simply the sum of all the parts of a system that possess one perfectly definite and absolutely uniform structure and com-

[1] Willard Gibbs, *Collected Papers*, i, p. 96.

position. A system, therefore, includes as many phases as it contains physically distinct varieties of homogeneous aggregation.

Beneath the phases are the components or primary constituents of the system. These were originally defined by Gibbs in a less elegant manner than the phases.[1] But by a slight modification in the mathematical development, which involves no change in the principles, components may be regarded as the several species of chemical substances, in so far as they are not decomposed, which are to be found in the system as a whole.[2] Every distinct variety of molecule, regardless of its physical state or states in the system, and regardless of the manner of its distribution throughout the system, provided only it is not liable to decomposition in this system, is a component.

Such is the generalized material composition of the system. It is characterized by two types of aggregation; the physical and the chemical. Each of these is to be logically analyzed into its several uniform constituent parts. These may be distributed or put together in the simplest or most complex manner. But there is never any theoretical difficulty in recognizing and distinguishing them.

[1] Willard Gibbs, *Collected Papers*, i, pp. 63 ff.
[2] Cf. Richards, *Journal of the American Chemical Society*, May, 1916.

More puzzling is the treatment of the system's energy or activity. It was chiefly in order to circumvent the difficulties here involved that Gibbs introduced the idea of isolation. His own preliminary statement best illustrates the nature of the case: " We will examine the conditions of equilibrium of a mass of matter of various kinds enclosed in a rigid and fixed envelop, which is impermeable to and unalterable by any of the substances enclosed, and perfectly non-conducting to heat. We will suppose that the case is not complicated by the action of gravity, or by any electrical influences, and that in the solid portions of the mass the pressure is the same in every direction. We will farther simplify the problem by supposing that the variations of the parts of the energy and entropy which depend upon the surfaces separating heterogeneous masses are so small in comparison with the variations of the parts of the energy and entropy which depend upon the quantities of these masses, that the former may be neglected by the side of the latter; in other words, we will exclude the considerations which belong to the theory of capillarity.

" It will be observed that the supposition of a rigid and non-conducting envelop enclosing the mass under discussion involves no real loss of generality, for if any mass of matter is in equilibrium, it would also be so, if the whole or any part of it were enclosed in an envelop as supposed; therefore the conditions of equilibrium for a mass thus enclosed are the general conditions which must always be satisfied in case of equilibrium. As for the other suppositions which have been made, all the circumstances and considerations which are here excluded will afterward be made the subject of special discussion." [1]

We need not follow such special discussions. It will suffice to note that all forms of energy and activity are involved in the definition of systems, but that temperature and pressure are of very general importance. Yet gravitation, which can never be screened, as well as electrical, magnetical, and optical phenomena, and all other activities may often be involved. Moreover if phases are finely divided as in colloidal systems, there will be a great increase in surface area, and capillary phenomena must ensue.

Another fundamental characteristic of a system is the magnitude of the concentration of each component in each phase. The recognition of this is perfectly essential to the description. But it is the last of the characteristics which must be taken into account in a system that has reached a state of equilibrium.

It is well, however, to go beyond Gibbs's discussion as presented in his formulation of the Phase

[1] *Loc. cit.*, p. 62.

Rule, and to note that so long as the condition of equilibrium has not been attained it is also necessary to take account of volume and configuration in the phases. With these discriminations the task is completed. Every physico-chemical aggregation as such, that is to say disregarding the functional relations of its parts as in a machine, the structural configuration as in a crystal, and the infra-molecular characteristics such as the nature of molecular structure or the phenomena of radio-active transformations, may thus be ideally described. Often, as in the living organism, the actual task presents insurmountable difficulties; but these difficulties are practical, rather than conceptual or ideal. And no one, not even the vitalist, doubts that the organism is a Gibbs system.

The difficulties involved in the use of this instrument of thought were recognized by no one more clearly than by Gibbs himself. They led him to his last and, as some of his pupils think, his most novel contribution to science, the work on Statistical Mechanics.[1] This book, written after long years of meditation, but, as it seems, almost without notes to aid in the task, and completed in a period of less than a year, is perhaps the greatest example of sustained thought in the history of America. Gibbs's motive in turning his attention

[1] New York, 1902.

in this direction is made clear in the preface, where, after pointing out discrepancies between thermodynamical theory and fact in the study of individual systems, he says: " Difficulties of this kind have deterred the author from attempting to explain the mysteries of nature, and have forced him to be contented with the more modest aim of deducing some of the more obvious propositions relating to the statistical branch of mechanics. Here, there can be no mistake in regard to the agreement of the hypotheses with the facts of nature, for nothing is assumed in that respect. The only error into which one can fall, is the want of agreement between the premises and the conclusions, and this, with care, one may hope, in the main, to avoid." [1]

The specific object of the inquiry, so original and daring as to be almost inconceivable to those who have not the advantage of Gibbs's insight into mathematics, is thus stated: " We may imagine a great number of systems of the same nature, but differing in the configurations and velocities which they have at a given instant, and differing not merely infinitesimally, but it may be so as to embrace every conceivable combination of configurations and velocities. And here we may set the problem, not to follow a particular system through its succession of configurations, but to determine how the

[1] *Loc. cit.*, p. x.

whole number of systems will be distributed among the various conceivable configurations and velocities at any required time, when the distribution has been given for some one time. The fundamental equation for this inquiry is that which gives the rate of change of the number of systems which fall within any infinitesimal limits of configuration and velocity." [1]

The undertaking seems to have been notably successful, for Gibbs goes on to say: " The laws of statistical mechanics apply to conservative systems of any number of degrees of freedom and are exact." [2] "The laws of thermodynamics may be easily obtained from the principles of statistical mechanics, of which they are the incomplete expression." [3]

" We may therefore confidently believe that nothing will more conduce to the clear apprehension of the relation of thermodynamics to rational mechanics, and to the interpretation of observed phenomena with reference to their evidence respecting the molecular constitution of bodies, than the study of the fundamental notions and principles of that department of mechanics to which thermodynamics is especially related." [4]

It is apparent, therefore, that Gibbs has provided physical science with a rigorous mathemati-

[1] *Loc. cit.*, p. vii.   [3] *Ibid.*, pp. viii, ix.
[2] *Ibid.*, p. ix.   [4] *Ibid.*, p. ix.

cal analysis of the conditions of equilibrium in any system and also in any ensemble of similar systems. I cannot pretend to understand more than a little of Gibbs's analysis, and regarding the interpretation of his statistical inquiry I am obliged to rely upon help from the mathematicians. Nor should I wish to be understood as venturing to accept or in any way to pass judgment on all of the results. The presumptions are solidly in their favor, but time alone can test the productions of even so great a man. Yet this is clearly the best that we now possess as a means to the general and abstract physico-chemical characterization of cosmic evolution, for it involves our general concepts of matter, energy, space, and time, it includes the one known law of evolution,[1] the second law of thermodynamics, as an implication of its own more general results, and it is, so far as we can now see, rigorous, exhaustive, and exact.

The results of Gibbs's thermodynamical studies clearly prove that Spencer's generalization bears no simple and intelligible relation to the laws of equilibrium. The Phase Rule may serve as an illustration of this fact. According to this rule the number of degrees of freedom, other things being equal, increases or diminishes as the number of phases diminishes or increases. In other words, roughly speaking, the greater the number of phases,

[1] Cf. Perrin, *Traité de chimie physique*, Paris, 1903, ch. 5.

the smaller is the number of kinds of variation which can occur in the system. This may be illustrated by the case of pure water. For example, in a system which consists of ice, water, and steam the composition of each phase, the temperature and the pressure are all absolutely fixed. And thus, compression or the addition or subtraction of heat from the outside can only change the quantities of the several phases until at length one of them may cease to exist, meanwhile leaving temperature, pressure and composition of the phases unchanged. But in the system of ice and water alone the application of pressure will at once produce a change in the pressure of the system, which will be accompanied by a change in the temperature. On the other hand, if either temperature or pressure be fixed in such a system, then the condition of the system is fully determined and the other factor — pressure or temperature as the case may be — cannot vary. A similar statement applies to the systems steam-water and steam-ice. Finally, if a system consists of the steam phase alone, it will not suffice to fix the temperature in order to fix the pressure, or vice versa. In order to fix the temperature it will be necessary to fix the pressure and the composition, i. e. the concentration or volume. And in like manner both temperature and pressure must be fixed in order to fix volume, both temperature and volume in order to fix pressure. The conditions for more complex systems are perfectly analogous.

Thus, at first sight, it appears that Spencer's idea of the greater stability of the multiform is justified. But a closer examination shows that his conception of multiformity involves not merely heterogeneity, or multiformity in phases, but also diversity in chemical composition and in the activities due to energy. At this point his views are radically contradicted by the Phase Rule. For the number of degrees of freedom increases by the same number as the number of components or different forms of energy which are involved in the system. Thus, if to the system steam-water-ice a little alcohol be added, there will result a system as variable as the simpler water-ice system. And the same thing is true if gravitation is appreciably involved in the original system. In short "the instability of the homogeneous" tends to reappear in the heterogeneous of Spencer though not in that of Gibbs.

It is now important that two facts should be well understood: (I) Other things being equal the stability of a system *increases* with the number of phases and also with the number of restrictions upon the intensities of energy, e. g. temperature, and upon the concentrations. Thus a system of three phases is more stable than a similar system of two phases; a system of constant temperature is more stable than a similar system in which the

temperature is variable; and a system in which
the tension of carbon dioxide is constant is more
stable than one in which this is a variable quantity.
(II) Other things being equal the stability of a system *diminishes* with increase of the number of its
undecomposed constituent molecular species, and
of the number of different forms of energy, e. g.
heat, pressure, electrical potential, surface tension,
which are involved in its activities.

Thus we must conclude that Spencer's view,
though not contradicted, is also not supported by
the Phase Rule. For while certain kinds of multiformity tend toward stability others tend toward
instability. Apparently the resultant of these two
tendencies in the phenomena of nature as a whole
can only be estimated by an objective consideration of the properties of matter. On this point we
may at once note that there is a general tendency
of the more complex molecular structures to instability, and that there is some reason to suppose
such a tendency to exist in the elements of greater
atomic weight. Moreover, complexity in the structure of a phase, whether through irregularity of its
configuration, or through its dispersion into separate fragments, is as a rule accompanied by a de-
crease of stability. But it is very doubtful if the
problem as a whole, in the present state of knowledge, can be solved. The Phase Rule indicates a
tendency toward the greater stability of a certain

kind of multiformity, which is exactly defined by Gibbs's term heterogeneity. But equally it proves other forms of multiformity to be unstable.

I cannot find any further support for Spencer's hypothesis in the results of Gibbs's Statistical Mechanics. And I think that we may admit, therefore, that the physicists' hostility to Spencer's theories has been well founded. Many of his views are indeed clearly in error, though, as a rule, from excessive generalization rather than from radical inconsistency with the elementary principles of science.

Spencer's belief in the tendency toward dynamic equilibrium in all things is of course fully justified. Its foundation may be discovered in the Phase Rule, and especially in the theorem of Le Chatelier.[1] But as formulated by Spencer this is nothing more than a return to Hume, and taken by itself this principle could never have served the purpose as a foundation for the Synthetic Philosophy.

[1] An interesting essay on the wide significance of this principle may be found in Bancroft's paper, *Journal of the American Chemical Society*, 1911, xxxiii, p. 92.

VIII

THE PROBLEM

HERBERT SPENCER'S *law of evolution* undoubtedly fails as a complete and rigorous principle, and it seems unlikely that any such law is for the present to be discovered. Yet, as we have seen, it is not altogether fallacious; nor is it without very substantial foundation in fact. As a general principle the instability of the homogeneous may be doubted and the invariable tendency to multiformity, as stated by Spencer, categorically denied. I am not sure, however, that the difficulty on the latter point may not be due to inconsistency between different statements in Spencer's own writings, and that so much of the idea as pervades his whole work, is better founded. In any case, there can be no doubt that he correctly analyzed many of the phenomena of nature. The extent to which he anticipated Darwin proves that. And it is certain that in the course of evolution at many points, perhaps even as a rule, there is a marked tendency toward differentiation and the production of complexity from that which is relatively simple. This is accompanied, moreover, by a uniform tendency toward equilibrium. In short, Spencer's "law" is a reasonably correct description of the evolutionary process.

The history of the earth clearly illustrates this. There was a time, according to an ancient theory now often disputed, when the earth was a molten mass, approximately homogeneous except for the continuous variations in the concentrations of the different elements which make it up, or possibly consisting of a small number of distinct phases. Provisionally adopting this theory, we perceive that this phase or these phases were enveloped in an atmosphere, likewise approximately homogeneous except for the influence of gravity upon the concentrations of the several constituents, which therefore made up a single gaseous phase. If the earth was once molten there is no other conclusion involved in remote geological and astronomical history so nearly certain as this, that the earth was once a two or three phase system. The few constituent phases were all, as phases go, of very unusual complexity ; first, because of the large number of components of the system, and secondly, because of the magnitude of the continuous variations in density and in concentrations throughout the phases. Such variations had been produced by gravitation.

This condition may be taken as the origin of terrestrial evolution. Of course this is a purely arbitrary proceeding, but any analysis of the nature of the evolutionary process must begin somewhere, and it had better begin not too far off in time and space, and with that condition which can be most probably made out.

The argument in favor of the belief that the earth was once in a thoroughly molten condition is moreover, from the physico-chemical standpoint, very strong, and certainly far stronger than that in favor of any one of the numerous complete cosmogonical hypotheses. This is perhaps best illustrated by the fact that none of the recognized theories of the origin of the earth appears to be radically inconsistent with such a view, while nearly all clearly involve this stage in the evolution of the earth.[1]

On any other assumption it is hard to see how the most general characteristics of the earth's crust, or the nature of the igneous rocks can be explained.[2] Further evidence is afforded by the molten condition of the sun and the stars, by the phenomena of vulcanism, and by many other considerations bearing on the present state of the interior of the earth, especially its great density. Finally, it is nothing short of fantastic to assume that the processes by which the earth was heated were just sufficient simultaneously to melt the whole mass, except a very thin crust. Such a coincidence can never be allowed without the support of arguments far more cogent than those which depend upon

[1] Cf. Poincaré, *Leçons sur les hypothèses cosmogoniques*, Paris, 1911.
[2] Cf. Daly, *Igneous Rocks*, chap. 8, New York, 1914.

any cosmogonical theory. Yet, without fusion how could the difference in density of surface and interior become established ? In truth, no hypothesis concerning the unknown past appears to be better founded than this hypothesis of a molten earth. It is established quite as securely as most of the scientific theories which are constantly employed without question. We are, however, only concerned with it provisionally as an hypothesis.

The conclusion that under these circumstances the earth must have consisted of a small number of phases rests upon experience. For the labors of the physical chemists conclusively prove the co-existence of a large number of liquid phases or of more than one gas phase to be impossible. The only restriction upon this statement is found in the case where mixing is incomplete. But though the size of the earth greatly restricts mixing, the long periods of time involved in geological processes must have gone far to neutralize such a tendency.

It is to be noted that the only current hypothesis that denies a molten epoch to the earth as such, assigns to the earth an origin by disruption from the molten sun. But to this early sun the above considerations equally apply.

Thus we reach a definite position: the earth, as such or as a part of the sun, was probably once in a molten state. Under these circumstances it is most conveniently regarded as a single system. This system consisted, for a long time, of a small number of phases of very great volume. These phases possessed one peculiar characteristic, for the force of gravity, even though opposed by diffusion, must have accomplished a differentiation with respect to the concentrations of the components at different levels throughout each phase. The components of this system were very numerous, in that they included at the very least all of the chemical elements. Conceivably certain chemical compounds which may happen to be quite stable at the temperature of the system may also have been involved as components. I think, however, that the existence of compounds which are undissociable at such temperatures may be regarded as unlikely. Possibly a few were present in the atmosphere. It is clear that we have thus imagined a condition of relative instability in the relatively homogeneous. Indeed, taking everything into consideration, the number of degrees of freedom must have been about one hundred. This may be compared with our laboratory systems where the number of degrees of freedom is rarely as great as ten. The instability of such a condition depends upon the fact that the number of components is large, while the number of phases is small.

Out of this condition the almost infinite variety of the present world has been evolved. We see about us countless systems — not indeed strictly independent, but nevertheless best conceived as such — which present the greatest diversity in respect of both phases and components. Such are the geological strata, the rocks, the sands, the soil, the lakes and streams, the ocean itself, and the atmosphere; and such is every living organism. We see, moreover, orderly relations between these systems.

It is evident that in the course of the evolution of the earth systems have evolved in great profusion, in inconceivable variety, with almost infinite diversity in phases, components, concentrations, and activities, and always in coördination. This indeed, abstractly stated, is the very essence of the evolutionary process. This is what evolution is. And we may now see that Herbert Spencer was not far wrong about it. Whatever may be the other peculiarities of the evolutionary process, relative stability in relative diversity has certainly succeeded relative instability in relative uniformity. And so it had to be if anything interesting (to introduce the teleological implication) was to happen. Apart from all theories regarding the formation of the crust, we shall soon see that this conclusion is established upon the foundation of geological fact.

It is now apparent, however, that the general laws of science do not sufficiently account for the evolution of the globe. The Phase Rule, the second law of thermodynamics, the principles of statis-

tical mechanics and the fact of the stability of
dynamic equilibria are all, like the laws of conservation and of gravitation, conditions of the process.
But the process itself is the evolution of the original
matter and the original energy of the globe. It is
the properties of this matter and of this energy
which chiefly bring to pass the manifold events in
the history of the earth, or at least which make it
possible that they should be manifold. Perhaps it
may be said that the above mentioned laws organ-
ize the historical events and the systems which
are the sole actors. But that which permits their
diversity, as thus organized, is the nature of the
matter and the energy themselves. Or, to put it
in another way, the characteristics of matter and
energy condition that to which the laws apply.
Spencer failed clearly to understand this, and therefore to establish his conclusions.

There is, perhaps, danger of making too much of
the antithesis between the laws of phenomena and
the characteristics of the various forms of matter
and manifestations of energy. Yet there is undoubtedly a certain logical priority in the law of
conservation of energy as compared with the phenomenon of an electric charge, or in Newton's law
of inverse squares as compared with the properties
of copper. This difference finds its expression in
the tendency of many thinkers to regard the laws
of conservation as necessary *a priori* truths, or to

consider Newton's law as a necessary consequence of the principles of geometry. A similar *a priori* character might easily be assigned to the second law of thermodynamics on account of its statistical foundation and, for similar reasons, to the tendency toward dynamic equilibrium. I am not here concerned to justify or to criticize this view, but to point out that no one is likely to take a similar position regarding the specific characteristics of things. Possibly the second law of thermodynamics, in one or another of its forms, might have been worked out by a mathematician in perfect ignorance of how energy should be conceived. This would hardly be a more remarkable achievement than the creation of non-Euclidian geometry; and in a way, it is not a bad description of Carnot's actual performance or of some of Gibbs's more finished productions. But no one can imagine the origin of the concept of an electrical charge until the phenomena of electricity had been investigated. In other words, the prediction of electrical phenomena by one ignorant of all such phenomena seems to be quite impossible.

Admitting that there is sufficient ground for a distinction, established solely for convenience and without philosophical implications, between the laws and the specific properties of things, we may now take another step. In the first place we note that the production of diversity would be impossible if matter and energy were uniform. It is because there are not far from a hundred elements, for the most part capable of entering into a great variety of chemical reactions, and because beside mechanical forces, there are many other ways in which energy manifests itself, that the world can become diversified. But this is far from sufficient as an analysis. For, secondly, we may note that if there were no tendency when solids are deposited from a molten mass to the separate formation of individual compounds, the process of evolution would hardly be more varied than the freezing of a huge mass of water. Thus we may vaguely perceive how the general and individual properties of matter and energy are alike concerned in the production of the manifold forms of nature.

So we have at length reached the real problem of the order of nature. Admitting that evolution consists in the evolution of systems, because systems make up the whole world of physical chemistry, we have to inquire in what manner the properties of matter and energy make possible that orderly diversity which is so conspicuous a result of the evolutionary process. The other characteristic result, the stability of the products of nature, we can more clearly see to be largely effected by the operation of natural laws. But we must not forget to consider this too. The question now arises: how far did the properties of matter and energy admit of freedom — using the word in its recognized scientific meaning — in the evolution of systems ?　To what extent, considering only these properties, are mere number, variety, and durability of systems possible ?　Or, in short, what are the properties of matter and energy which must be taken into consideration when we regard them as material for the construction of systems and of ensembles of systems of every kind, i. e. of *any* kind ?　I hope that a knowledge of the character of Willard Gibbs's researches may make this question seem not quite illusory.

In this inquiry it will be necessary to take account of number, of diversity, and of durability in systems as a whole, in their phases, their components, their concentrations, and in all the forms of their activity.　Further, in that the concept of isolation is a fiction, it will be necessary to consider relations between systems, thus introducing the ideas of pattern and organization.　But nothing else need be considered.　For these are the primary qualities of the world, established at length by the analysis of modern science after centuries of vain philosophizing.

It must not be supposed that the problem of the coöperation of the laws of nature has disappeared in the course of our analysis, nor that it has been solved.　This is still a genuine problem and an open question.　Yet I think it is less promising than that of the coöperation of the properties of matter and energy. At any rate there is nothing to hinder us from now disregarding it. For we have arrived at a clear issue which is open to an independent examination.

Nearly all the phenomena of the evolution of the earth have taken place upon the surface during the existence of the crust. This fact is a necessary consequence of the principles of physical science just examined. For the evolution of systems could only begin on a large scale with the intervention of solid phases. There was, however, one great process that involved not the crust only, but the whole earth, and lead to a partial separation of the chemical elements under the action of the force of gravitation.

It is not unlikely that this separation depended especially upon the existence of just two liquid phases in the molten earth; — a central metallic core and an outer slag. Such conditions would correspond to the state of affairs in a blast furnace. The structure of meteorites, moreover, seems to be consistent with such a two-phase origin, and I know not what other physico-chemical explanation can be suggested.[1]

Thus, or otherwise, the lighter elements have come to the surface in relatively great quantities.

[1] These considerations were suggested to me by Professor T. W. Richards. I cannot think that a physically and chemically intelligible alternative hypothesis has yet been made out.

Moreover, such differentiation into phases as had always existed since the earth somehow became a large dense aggregate involved the existence of an atmosphere. In this atmosphere great quantities of certain elements, all of them also relatively light, which could exist free or in combination as stable gases under the existing conditions, were present.

Thus it has come about that only a few of the elements, and those as a rule of low atomic weights, have had a large part in the evolutionary processes. Such are hydrogen, carbon, nitrogen, oxygen, sodium, magnesium, aluminium, silicon, chlorine, calcium, and iron. We may at once note the fact that the elements of low atomic weight are generally more intense and more diverse in their chemical activity. In this manner the very earliest stages of differentiation have led to an increase in the possibilities of chemical changes during the course of the evolutionary process. It must not be supposed, however, that any elements have thus been excluded from the crust. The effect of these processes has been only to alter the distribution of the elements in the manner indicated, and to produce a relatively light exterior and a relatively dense interior of the lithosphere.

While the formation of the earth's crust was proceeding and thereafter until the present time the atmosphere has persisted. Meanwhile it has undergone great changes in composition so that its early history is little known. But in its composition the lightest of the important elements — hydrogen, carbon, nitrogen, and oxygen — have never failed in recent times. For a long period, certainly since an early stage of organic evolution, these elements have existed in the forms of chemical combination, if not in the proportions, in which they are now present in the air, viz., as water, carbon dioxide, nitrogen, and oxygen. Still earlier, for a very long period, at least water, carbon dioxide, and nitrogen were present.

As the cooling of the earth progressed a temperature was finally reached at which water began to condense out of the atmosphere. Before that time the differentiation of systems upon the earth's surface had been in steady progress. Igneous rocks had been formed. They had probably been torn and twisted in their structure and variously segregated by volcanic upheavals and other great changes. But such processes are as nothing to those which were to follow. For water is the most powerful and most universal agent in moulding the surface of the earth. The meteorological cycle resulted from the precipitation of water, and has continued, presumably without interruption, until the present time.

Any objection which may be felt to the above provisional account of early geological processes may now be readily obviated. For it is possible to look back with certainty at least to the earlier epochs of the meteorological cycle. At that time the crust of the earth, however differentiated into systems as compared with a molten sphere, was still almost perfectly homogeneous or at least disorganized if contrasted with its present condition. For all finer comminution and all the organic phenomena are later in epoch, and there were then no intricate orderly relations between the different systems. From this point, no less than from the earlier hypothetical single system, the process of the evolution of systems has steadily gone on in the general manner which has been above remarked, or, in other words, more or less according to the requirements of Spencer's " law."

In the course of the meteorological cycle the movements of water became canalized. Streams, lakes, and the ocean assumed a somewhat definite form, water began to penetrate the débris resulting from its own action, and from that of dissolved carbonic acid, to set this in motion, and thus in certain localities to form deposits. Some of these have become strata, others, with the help of further agencies, earth and soil. And at length nearly everything that meets the eye, except life and the products of life, has been moulded into its form by the action of water and carbonic acid.

The only other great event in the history of the earth — but of this we have no knowledge — is the beginning of the process of organic evolution. Yet if the meteorological processes have multiplied a thousand fold the evolution of systems, organic evolution has again multiplied these in a like proportion. The elements here chiefly involved are, once more, hydrogen, carbon, nitrogen, and oxygen.

Thus what is known with certainty about the history of the earth enables us to see that a few elements, and especially the four organic ones, are the chief factors. Among these nitrogen plays a somewhat subordinate rôle, especially in the mineral kingdom, while hydrogen, carbon, and oxygen, notably as constituents of water and carbon dioxide, are almost everywhere of equal importance.

This conclusion admits of another advance in the analysis and a final formulation of the problem. We have noted, step by step, that Gibbs's abstract concept of system is a means to the exhaustive characterization of the world as contemplated by physical chemistry: that systems are made up of phases and components: that these are characterized by the concentrations of the components in the phases, and by the various manifestations of energetic activity: and that in certain cases volume and configuration must also be regarded. We have also seen that the process of evolution of the

earth appears, when examined in the light of this
concept, as a continuous production of many systems related together in an orderly manner from
few original systems, and that these systems are
not only very numerous but also very diverse and
often very stable. Further, we have seen that
there is ground for the belief that the more important conditions which make possible this evolutionary process are the specific characteristics of
matter and energy as they coöperate in the process, rather than the most general laws of physical
science. And at length we have discovered that
the elements which, by the combination of their
characteristic properties and activities, chiefly
make possible the greater part of the results of the
evolutionary process are but three — hydrogen,
carbon, and oxygen.

Now we may ask what is the relation of the properties and activities of hydrogen, carbon, and
oxygen as causes to the evolution of numerous,
diverse, stable systems as effects ?   How is it that,
on account of the peculiarities of these three elements, there are so many degrees of freedom left
open in the evolutionary process ? This is the
question which will be discussed in the following
pages. I have already examined it in a less systematic manner in *The Fitness of the Environment*. I hope now to simplify and to generalize the
analysis.

IX

THE THREE ELEMENTS

COMPONENTS

OF all the chemical elements, hydrogen, carbon, and oxygen possess the greatest number of compounds and enter into the greatest variety of reactions. The known compounds of carbon, which very often contain all three elements, are numbered by ten thousands, while the possible carbon compounds are almost innumerable. The compounds of inorganic chemistry in a very large number of cases also contain oxygen or hydrogen. Thus these elements afford by far the greatest number of components for the constitution of systems.

This unique combining power of the three elements with other elements, but especially among themselves, depends of course upon their very nature, upon those characteristics which are peculiar to them and mark them off from all other elements. These properties, moreover, produce characteristics in the compounds which distinguish these from the compounds of other elements. Thus the compounds of oxygen are commonly very reactive, the compounds of carbon with hydrogen, taking account of the size of the molecule, very stable. But, in a somewhat less conspicuous manner, numerous other elements present similar phenomena, and the most striking chemical property of the three elements is therefore the variety of their combinations.

The necessary condition for the number and diversity of carbon compounds is the ability of the single atom of carbon to combine with several other atoms, actually with four, and thus, according to the atomic theory, to make possible the formation of chains, forked chains, and rings of atoms in the molecule. But this fact of the quadrivalence of carbon is in itself by no means unique, nor is it evident that a combining power of four is necessarily better than five. What is remarkable is the ability of chains and rings of carbon atoms to hold together, especially when hydrogen is the principal other element of the molecular structure. The history of chemistry indicates that this is a unique phenomenon, for in our experience it is not paralleled.

Compounds of hydrogen and carbon, free from all other elements, and therefore known as hydrocarbons, exist in the most bewildering profusion. One such compound probably possesses a straight chain of sixty carbon atoms, and there is no reason to suppose that chemists have approached the limit of length of such chains. Moreover, these may

apparently be forked at any point, they may be
joined into a great number of ring systems, and
rings and chains of all kinds may be combined
within a single molecular structure. Finally, more
than one valence of each of the carbon atoms may,
as it seems, be involved in the union between two
such atoms. A single example of molecular structure expressed according to current theories may
serve to illustrate these considerations.

It is, however, hardly possible briefly to give a fair
account of the number and diversity of such substances. Hundreds are known and the possibility
of the existence of countless thousands is fully
established.

When oxygen is introduced into such structures
the number and still more the variety of the compounds is thereby further multiplied. For the
different types of union of oxygen with hydrocarbons produce alcohols, aldehydes and ketones,

acids, ethers, esters, and many other classes of bodies. Thus, among the millions of possible compounds which are made up exclusively of the three elements hydrogen, carbon, and oxygen, there are many different kinds of substances which possess a great variety of physical and chemical properties. Further combinations with other elements, especially with nitrogen which is always present in the air, still more complicate the conditions, so that a brief account of all the compounds of organic chemistry is quite impossible.[1]

In order to estimate the importance of this subject it is necessary to consider two facts. In the first place the elements of low atomic weight possess an especially marked chemical individuality, so that there is reason to suppose that no other elements closely resemble hydrogen, carbon, and oxygen in this or in any other specific chemical property. Secondly, there can be no doubt that carbon and hydrogen fit together in a peculiar manner and therefore produce stable aggregates of atoms. This may be seen in an important fact which has been unaccountably neglected: the substitution of a hydrocarbon radical for hydrogen in a molecule, like the substitution of one hydrocarbon radical for another, has little effect upon the properties of the compound. But the substi-

---

[1] Cf. *The Fitness of the Environment*, pp. 196–209. All the following references in this chapter are to the same book.

tution of anything else for one of these radicals usually produces a complete change in physical and chemical properties. This may be illustrated by the so-called ionization constants of certain organic acids, which serve to measure their acid strength.

Substance	Formula	Ionization Constant
Acetic acid	$CH_3.COOH$	0.000018
Propionic acid	$CH_3.CH_2.COOH$	0.000014
Butyric acid	$CH_3.CH_2.CH_2.COOH$	0.000016
Glycolic acid	$CH_2OH.COOH$	0.00015
Chloracetic acid	$CH_2Cl.COOH$	0.0015
Dichloracetic acid	$CHCl_2.COOH$	0.05
Trichloracetic acid	$CCl_3.COOH$	1.2
Glycocoll	$CH_2NH_2.COOH$	0.00000000018
Oxalic acid	$COOH.COOH$	0.1

Moreover, the very system of classification of organic chemistry depends upon putting together all compounds which differ in respect only of hydrocarbon radicals (i. e. such radicals as are made up of the elements hydrogen and carbon exclusively) and separating all compounds which differ structurally in any other respect whatsoever. Thus, for example, acetic acid $CH_3.COOH$, and stearic acid, $CH_3.CH_2.CH_2.CH_2.CH_2.CH_2.CH_2.CH_2.-CH_2.CH_2.CH_2.CH_2.CH_2.CH_2.CH_2.CH_2.CH_2.COOH$ belong to the same homologous series of compounds, while alcohol, $CH_3.CH_2OH$ belongs to another series. This method of classification is one of the most successful and perfect in existence, for, though founded on theory, in very large measure it fits the facts, bringing together those bodies which in their chemical behavior belong together, and separating such as are chemically unlike. But this can only be due to something very near to chemical equivalence between hydrogen and the various hydrocarbon radicals. This is especially true of the paraffine radicals, less so with the others. Nevertheless, except for the influence of the mere size of the molecule, the compound toluene, C_6H_5-CH_3, resembles methane, CH_4, more than methyl alcohol, CH_3OH, does. This condition finds its expression in the fact that such compounds as the paraffine hydrocarbons

$$
\begin{array}{ccccc}
\text{H} & \text{CH}_3 & \text{CH}_3 & \text{CH}_3 & \text{CH}_3 \\
| & | & | & | & | \\
\text{H--C--H} & \text{H--C--H} & \text{H--C--H} & \text{H--C--CH}_3 & \text{H}_3\text{C--C--CH}_3 \\
| & | & | & | & | \\
\text{H} & \text{H} & \text{CH}_3 & \text{CH}_3 & \text{CH}_3
\end{array}
$$

are almost identical in properties, except for the effect of the size of the molecule, while none of the oxygen derivatives of methane,

$$
\begin{array}{ccccc}
\text{H} & \text{H} & \text{H} & \text{OH} & \text{OH} \\
| & | & | & | & | \\
\text{H--C--H} & \text{H--C--OH} & \text{H--C--OH} & \text{H--C--OH} & \text{HO--C--OH} \\
| & | & | & | & | \\
\text{H} & \text{H} & \text{OH} & \text{OH} & \text{OH}
\end{array}
$$

although no greater percentage change in composition is involved in their formation, closely resembles any other in any respect. It is not customary to state the facts of organic chemistry in this manner, but the whole science shows that there is a close resemblance between hydrogen and hydrocarbon radicals when they are both joined to carbon atoms.

Accordingly, there is no reason to doubt the evidence of all chemical experience that organic chemistry is a unique field and that other elements cannot enter into a like number and variety of combinations.[1]

In forming the organic substances of which they are composed, plants and animals disclose chemical powers of the most admirable nature, which are quite beyond our present ability to imitate or even to explain. Yet, if it were not for one fact, it is hardly conceivable that life, with all its activity and complexity, could have thoroughly established itself in chemical mechanism. This fact is the simple chemical relationship between the primary constituents of the environment, water and carbonic acid, and the carbohydrates. It is a truism that if anything is to be done with water and carbonic acid as materials for organic synthesis, oxygen must be partially separated from hydrogen and carbon. When this is accomplished, substances result which are closely related to the carbohydrates, and which in some instances spontaneously form monosaccharides. The carbohydrates, which thus constitute a natural pathway from the inorganic to the organic, are in many respects of the

---

[1] *Loc. cit.*, pp. 191–221.

highest interest. Not only do they include a great variety of substances, widely different in properties, such as glucose, cane sugar, starch, cellulose, etc., but, as the researches of Lobry de Bruyn, Nef, and others have shown, their chemical reactivity is simply unparalleled. Thus, for example, a faintly alkaline solution of glucose, such as may exist in sea water, if left to itself will sooner or later contain probably more than two hundred different substances, all of them chemically active, belonging to a large number of different classes of compounds, and in many instances capable of entering into reactions with a great variety of other bodies. In this manner the course of inorganic evolution has provided substances which are directly available as materials for the production of many of the infinitely varied organic substances. Under these circumstances it is not surprising that carbohydrates are in fact the primary products of agriculture and of plant synthesis in general.[1]

One of the commonest reactions of organic substances is hydrolysis, a chemical transformation in which water, naturally associated with all organic products, is involved. This process possesses certain peculiarities which are significant for the present discussion. Hydrolysis is free from appreciable transformations of energy, and, as a result, it is usually a quiet process which runs without the

[1] *Loc. cit.*, pp. 222–232.

complication of side reactions to a condition of equilibrium. It is, therefore, readily controlled and adjusted at different end points, or reversed. In this manner, under natural conditions, a great variety of chemical changes are made possible, which may be perfectly regulated and carried out with the greatest economy. No doubt partly for these reasons reactions of hydrolysis are almost the commonest of bio-chemical processes.[1]

Taking all these facts into consideration, it may now be seen that the constituent elements of water and carbon dioxide are the best sources of components of systems; that the pathway from the simple compounds of the atmosphere to the complex organic bodies is a direct one; and that natural conditions facilitate the working over of the organic products, often without appreciable loss of material or of energy, in a great many different ways.

This, however, is but a part of the case, for the chemical activity of hydrogen and oxygen is not less conspicuous among the compounds of inorganic chemistry, that is to say, in their reactions with all the other elements. A large proportion of all inorganic compounds contain one or both of these elements; they are present in the great majority of the more common and important compounds; and they are especially conspicuous in the most active and important reagents. Thus, it is

[1] *Loc. cit.*, pp. 232–237.

evident that each and all of the three elements, hydrogen, carbon, and oxygen, possess peculiar chemical activity and that their simultaneous presence is essential to the production of the greatest possible number of different chemical substances as components of systems.[1]

Equally significant in the course of evolution has been the effect of water and carbonic acid in mobilizing all the elements of the earth's crust. From the beginning of the meteorological cycle this process has gone on. It has been efficient for many reasons. In the first place, water is the best of all solvents.[2] Secondly, carbonic acid, because of the precise degree of its solubility, everywhere accompanies water and enhances its action until, on account of the precise degree of its strength as an acid, a small amount of dissolved basic material effectually neutralizes the acid, without, however, chemically combining with more than a portion of it. For this reason carbon dioxide cannot be completely locked up in chemical combination, just as it cannot be physically extracted from the air or water.[3]

The circulation of water, which is the necessary condition for such action, depends for its rapidity, if not for its very existence, upon the fact that the vapor tension of water varies greatly, indeed more

[1] *Loc. cit.*, pp. 237–243. [2] *Loc. cit.*, pp. 111 ff.
[3] This subject is more fully discussed below, pp. 168, 169.

than that of any other substance, with the temperature.[1] Thus the precipitation of rain and dew and the process of evaporization are both greatly enhanced. It would seem that a substance of ordinary properties might hardly circulate at all as water does upon the surface of the earth. Finally, it is to be observed that the surface tension, which is greater than that of any other common liquid except mercury, causes water to remain in the soil or wherever capillary phenomena are possible, and thus prolongs the action of water as a solvent.[2]

In this manner all elements have been uncovered and set in motion by water. Many of them have been dissolved and carried down to the sea where they still remain dissolved in enormous quantities. Every mineral has been disintegrated, ground to dust, and dispersed by the streams and winds. For countless ages, prodigious quantities of all the elements have been thus in motion all over the earth. At present the yearly run-off of the rivers of the globe is believed to be about 6,500 cubic miles, and the dissolved material nearly five billion tons, to say nothing of the sediment.

Especially in the ocean the result of this process to make the various elements available is evident. Here may be found in solution almost half of all the elements, in appreciable amounts, making up a total mass of nearly 500,000,000,000,000,000

[1] *Loc. cit.*, pp. 104–105.   [2] *Loc. cit.*, pp. 126 ff.

tons, dissolved in more than 10,000,000,000,000,-
000,000 tons of water. This vast accumulation
depends upon the fact that water not only dissolves
many substances, but is able to hold great quantities of them in solution. In this respect, too, it
is unsurpassed by other liquids.[1]

As a result of the process of ionization, all of
these dissolved substances enter into chemical
reactions with one another. Thus the variety of
chemical compounds present in sea water is much
increased. Here, again, the properties of water are
important, for when we consider both the extent
to which ionizing substances can dissolve in water,
and their degree of ionization when they are dissolved, it is evident that this process is far more
extensive in aqueous solution than under any other
circumstances.[2]

Taking account of all the above considerations,
it is apparent that water is more widely distributed
over the surface of the earth than any other substance could be, that it everywhere carries carbonic
acid with it; that when it disappears from a local-
ity it is, on account of the rapidity of circulation,
more rapidly renewed than would be the case if it
possessed other properties, but also that it persists
longer in many localities on account of its high
surface tension, and elsewhere on account of the
high latent heats of fusion and of evaporation,

[1] *Loc. cit.*, pp. 171 ff.   [2] *Loc. cit.*, pp. 118 ff.

than could anything else. Moreover, it more effectively dissolves and comminutes all the constituents of the earth's crust than would be possible if its properties and those of carbonic acid were different from what they are. It stores up the greatest possible variety and quantity of material in the sea, holding this permanently in solution, and on account of its electrical properties, affording the conditions of ionic reactions in the greatest variety. Thus the properties of water condition all over the earth the formation of other components beside those which belong to organic chemistry, in an unparalleled number and variety and in vast quantity.

Therefore it may be said that the unique properties of hydrogen, carbon, and oxygen, of water and carbon dioxide, are uniquely favorable to the existence of the greatest possible number, variety, and quantity of components of systems.

PHASES

Phases are constituted of components. Therefore it is evident that all the preceding facts apply to phases and components alike. But there is more to the phase than the components which make it up, for the concept of phase includes that of component plus something more, just as the concept system involves something more than the sum of the phases.

In the first place, the phase has its quantitative as well as its qualitative characteristics; in short, concentrations are involved. Now water, as already explained, can dissolve a larger variety of substances in greater concentrations than any other liquid. Hence, the possible variations of water phases far exceed those of any other liquid phase. The liquids of the organism bear evidence upon this subject, and nothing is more certain than that the process of organic evolution would be very greatly restricted if water were not at hand as a means to incorporate solid substances. As a vehicle, of course, water here plays the same rôle as in the geological processes, with the same success, for the same reasons.[1]

One particular case of concentration, that of the second primary constituent of the environment, viz., carbonic acid, in the first, viz., water, is of special importance. This has already been mentioned, and must now be more fully explained. The solubility of gaseous carbon dioxide in pure water is such that at a temperature a little below 20° Centigrade, when equilibrium has been established between a gas mixture containing carbon dioxide and a water phase in contact with the gas, the amount of carbon dioxide in a given volume of the water will be just equal to the amount remaining in the same volume of the gas. At the freezing

[1] *Loc. cit.*, pp. 111–118.

point water will hold nearly twice as much carbon dioxide as the air; at 40° about half as much; at the boiling point, about one-fourth as much. Accordingly, at such temperatures as necessarily obtain during the existence of an ocean, free carbon dioxide must always be rather evenly distributed between the air and the waters of the globe. Water can never wash the carbonic acid out of the air, nor the air extract it from the water. No other common gas shares this property. Thus throughout nature the aqueous phases always contain carbonic acid and as a result the three elements are everywhere available for synthesis of organic substances. This property of carbon dioxide has been one of the most important factors in organic evolution. It has made possible the growth of forests on the mountains, and, in the process of metabolism, it has enabled the higher animals to dispose of quantities of carbonic acid that would otherwise be quite beyond their powers.

When this gas dissolves in water it forms carbonic acid, properly so called, H_2CO_3, and thus an acid reaction is produced. This acid reaction is largely responsible for the solvent power of rain water upon the majority of minerals. But after a small portion of the free acid has combined with basic material, the acidity of the solution is reduced to an insignificant value, and thereafter great variations in the relative amounts of acid and base have very little effect upon the reaction. In order to understand this fact it is necessary to know that the acidity of an aqueous solution is measured by its concentration of hydrogen ions. When the concentration of these is approximately one part in ten billion parts of water, the reaction is neutral. If the concentration be higher the reaction is acid, if lower, it is alkaline. The most weakly acid solutions of the laboratory possess hydrogen ion concentrations many thousands times greater than this quantity and the most weakly alkaline solutions proportionally lower concentrations. But when a solution of carbonic acid contains an amount of the base equivalent to only two or three per cent of the total acid, its hydrogen ion concentration is only about one hundred times as great as that which marks the neutral point. If base be added to such a solution the reaction will become very gradually less acid and more alkaline until, when at length a mere fraction of a per cent of the acid remains free, the alkalinity finally amounts to one hundred times the value at the neutral point. Thus all natural waters and the organism itself possess a nearly neutral reaction which can hardly be disturbed except by the addition of enormous quantities of acid or alkali.

The concentration of the hydrogen ion is thus regulated by carbonic acid throughout nature as it could not be by a substance possessing even

slightly different properties in respect of solubility
or as an acid. When it is remembered that the
hydrogen ion and the hydroxyl ion, whose concentration is inversely proportional to that of the
hydrogen ion, are the most generally active constituents of aqueous solutions the importance of
the conditions above explained, both for inorganic
and for organic evolution, may be understood,[1] for
thus the effective regulation of the most important
chemical variables of aqueous solutions is made
possible.

There is one characteristic of phases which is
probably more important than all others as a
means to produce complexity of systems. This is
comminution or dispersion into minute discrete
aggregates. Such a condition exists in the soil,
and it has been already remarked that the great
surface tension of water enables the soil to obtain
and to hold water more readily than would be
otherwise possible. But in typically colloidal systems, where the dispersion is still more complete
and the separate particles still smaller, surface
tension is at least as important as in the soil. There
is, moreover, hardly a possibility that life should
manifest itself except in colloidal systems, for no
other material aggregates even remotely approach
these in complexity. However that may be, the

---

[1] For a full treatment of this question, a broader explanation must
be consulted. This may be found in Chapter IV of *The Fitness of the
Environment.*

unique surface tension of water is highly favorable
to colloidal phenomena wherever they may occur.[1]

We have now seen that the properties of the
three elements not only make possible the greatest
diversity of phases, but also favor high concentrations, everywhere determine a high concentration
of carbon dioxide, regulate the concentrations of
hydrogen and hydroxyl ions, and promote the
existence of colloidal systems. Once more these
results depend upon the existence of a unique
group of singular characteristics. If one of these
characteristics were lacking, the whole process of
evolution would be less than it is, and organic evolution might be reduced to almost nothing. It
should not be forgotten that no valid objection to
this conclusion can be founded upon the possibility
of another kind of organic evolution. For, though
the organisms might well be different from what
they are, and certainly must be so upon another
planet, every organism is always a system, and its
complexity, like its other characteristics, must
therefore be that of a system.

ACTIVITIES

It is in systems that all forms of activity manifest
themselves. Therefore, any form of activity may
be produced by a suitable system. Accordingly,
those conditions which make possible the greatest

[1] *Loc. cit.*, pp. 126–130.

variety of systems also favor the greatest variety of activities, whether physical or chemical, electrical or mechanical. But, for activity, energy is also necessary.

Chemical substances, as such, liberate energy through chemical transformations. Therefore, in considering the elements as sources of energy, it is first necessary to take account of the energy transformations which accompany their reactions. Every chemical reaction involves simultaneous rearrangements of matter and energy. The latter quantity is most conveniently measured as the heat of reaction. The first fact which now arises is that oxygen of all elements possesses, in general, the highest heats of reaction; and as has been explained, this element combines with a greater variety of substances than does any other element. Moreover, the heat of reaction of oxygen with hydrogen far surpasses that of any other oxidation while the heat of oxidation of carbon is only less important. Finally, the great variety of reactions possible among all the compounds of hydrogen, carbon, and oxygen involve the possibility of an equal variety of energy transformations. Accordingly, the three elements are no less uniquely favorable as means to render energy available and thus to activate systems than they are for the production of the systems which are to be activated.[1]

[1] *Loc. cit.*, pp. 243–247.

The great source of energy upon the earth is solar radiation as it is made available in the meteorological cycle. We have already seen that a number of the unique properties of water combine to render this process more active and therefore a richer source of energy than would be otherwise possible. For here, other things being equal, the energy transformed is proportional to the rate of circulation. It may also be noted that another source of activity, the wind, also depends upon the properties of water, while ocean currents depend on winds. Finally, it is hardly necessary to say that tides can endure only while the ocean persists.

In the present state of natural science it is not possible systematically to analyze the conditions of the production of all different forms of activity. We must be content with the observation that solar energy is in fact transformed physically through the circulation of water, and chemically through the synthetic process in the leaf, into a great variety of forms. Thus activity upon the earth has become widespread, varied, and intense.

There are, however, two further special instances of activity which can be clearly understood as the result of the peculiar properties of water. When water evaporates the heat of vaporization is rendered latent, as the older physics had it. This latent heat of vaporization of water is far greater than any other latent heat of vaporization. In like manner latent heat is involved in the melting of ice, to a degree unsurpassed except by the latent heat of fusion of ammonia. When water vapor condenses and when water freezes the latent heat is once more liberated. Thus two processes that take place all over the earth are accompanied by enormous transformations of energy. These processes are of course mere incidents of the meteorological cycle.[1]

The second special instance of activity is to be found in the process of ionization. As a result of this phenomenon, electrical charges are produced. And because the process of ionization is more important in water than in other liquids, this source of electrical activity is unsurpassed.

These two phenomena, like the circulation of water, the synthesis of carbohydrate in the leaf, and the combustion of all organic substances, once more depend upon unique properties of the elements, and therefore themselves possess unique properties.

Systems

The stability of environmental conditions is necessary to the duration of systems. Such stability is a very conspicuous characteristic of the surface of the earth, and is by no means solely due to the natural tendency to the establishment and

---

[1] *Loc. cit.*, pp. 92 ff.

preservation of dynamic equilibrium. Here again
the properties of the three elements are of primary
importance.

Chemically the inertness of the natural waters
when dissolved carbonic acid is balanced by bicar-
bonates constitutes a most important factor in this
stability. For into such a fluid almost all substances may enter without suffering modification.
Hence, as a medium, water is neutral and inert.
Another factor of stability is the effective mixing
of the ocean which results from numerous unique
properties of water itself, such as the coefficient of
expansion, excessive evaporization in the tropics
and excessive precipitation in the polar regions —
processes which are continuous only because of
meteorological circulation. The ocean currents,
both superficial and deep, are also involved. Thus
it comes about that the ocean is nearly constant in
concentration, in composition, and in alkalinity.[1]

In many respects such subjects have already
incidentally been discussed; in others, they may
perhaps be sufficiently explained by considering
the regulation of temperature on the earth. For
this process is of special importance and involves
a large number of other regulatory phenomena.
The most obvious, though not the most important
factor in restricting the fluctuations of temperature,
both locally and generally all over the surface of

[1] *Loc. cit.*, chapter V.

the earth, is the heat capacity, or specific heat of water. This quantity is greater than in the case of any other common liquid except ammonia. As a result, when a body of water gains or loses heat, the change of its temperature is relatively very slight. In this manner the temperature of the ocean and of lakes and streams is stabilized, while the living organism is enabled to produce great quantities of heat without unduly elevating its temperature.[1] Still more striking in certain circumstances is the effect of the latent heats of fusion and of vaporization. The latent heat of vaporization is perhaps the chief factor in moderating the summer temperatures of islands and of the seaboard. Moreover, the heat thus rendered latent is liberated again in other, and on the whole, colder localities when the vapor is once more liquefied as rain and dew. The very high heat absorption which accompanies the evaporation of water is also a precious if not an indispensable factor in cooling animals and plants. And it possesses the further advantage that the process is more rapid the higher the temperature. Thus the greater tendency of the temperature to rise the greater is the cooling effect of evaporation. No other substance approaches the efficiency of water in these respects. The very high latent heat of melting tends in like manner to check the fall of

[1] *Loc. cit.*, pp. 80 ff.

temperature in the waters of the earth and in their neighborhood, while the relatively high freezing point brings this process into action at a temperature where chemical activity is still considerable.

Both of the high latent heats also operate very effectively to preserve bodies of water. Thus an enormous quantity of heat is necessary in order completely to evaporate away a lake or pond, and a smaller but still very large quantity must be given up before such a body of water can freeze throughout its whole extent. Certain other factors are even more effective to prevent the complete solidification of bodies of water. The well known anomalous expansion of fresh water near the freezing point brings the coldest water to the surface and prevents loss of heat from the warmer water below except through conduction, an ineffective process, or mechanical mixing, an uncommon one. The ice, once formed upon the surface, is kept there by its buoyancy, and thus an almost perfect protection of the liquid water below is established.

It is to be observed that though the ability of water to conduct heat is low, it is none the less larger than that of nonmetallic substances in general and a maximum for common liquids. Conduction is always unimportant as a means to regulate the temperature of large bodies of liquids, but in small aggregates like cells, where convection is restricted, this process is probably of great importance. In cells another property of water, the very high mobility of its molecules, although this has been overlooked by physiologists, is also of great significance.

In the ocean the properties of water produce the greatest constancy of temperature, just as they there lead to constancy of composition and concentration, to a rich, varied and universally available supply of the chemical elements and, through the coöperation of carbonic acid, to constancy of reaction. More than anything else the ocean embodies the characteristics of the three elements, and therefore reveals their value as a means to promote the existence of systems.

The ocean, however, affords but one example of the manner in which the several factors of evolution, in so far as they depend upon the three elements, form themselves into conditions which facilitate the evolutionary process. On every hand other examples may be seen. But it is unnecessary further to pursue this subject, for the facts which are important in the present inquiry have now been set forth.

X

THE TELEOLOGICAL ORDER

OUR scientific examination of the properties and activities of the three elements may now be made to serve its purpose. For it has led to results that can be used in answering the question of the origin of the teleological appearance of nature. Though we are still a very long way from a complete solution of the whole problem, we have found that which may yield an answer to the restricted form of that inquiry which a preliminary analysis has led us to consider.

It will be remembered that the complete question was found to be insoluble, except through an exhaustive description of all the details of the evolutionary process. This was recognized to be impossible. From this the necessity of treating the subject abstractly followed as a conclusion. Further considerations led to the view that the laws of nature provide an imperfect but yet intelligible account of certain general characteristics of orderliness in the phenomena of nature and the products of evolution. These principles, however, give no account of the origin of diversity. It was apparent that diversity must especially depend upon the existence and availability of suitable structural materials in the necessary profusion, variety, and stability; upon the existence of conditions which preserve these structures; and upon wealth of forces which form and activate them. Such specifications, like those of an architect or an engineer, concern the properties of matter and energy, rather than the laws of nature.

The ensemble of properties of the elements hydrogen, carbon, and oxygen, meet most of these specifications. They lead, as we have seen, to the presence of water and carbon dioxide in the atmosphere, and to the meteorological cycle. This cycle regulates the temperature of the globe more perfectly than it could be regulated by any other substances concerned in any other similar cycle. It produces an almost constant temperature in the ocean, as well as constancy of composition and of alkalinity. It mobilizes all over the earth great quantities of all the elements; it deposits them in great variety and inexhaustible profusion in the ocean; it comminutes and disperses all kinds of insoluble minerals, thereby diversifying the land; it causes water to penetrate and to remain in nearly all localities; and all of these processes are more perfect or more extensive than they could be if a large number of the different properties of water were not what they are. Thereby the greatest variety and quantity of structual materials is accumulated. Meanwhile the conditions which make for durability of structures are also assured.

Other similar results depend upon the chemical properties of these three elements. Such properties lead to an even greater variety of chemical combinations and chemical reactions, to an unequaled diversity of properties in their products, and to qualitatively and quantitatively important transformations of energy.

Out of all these substances, inorganic and organic alike, as a result of the properties of water and of carbon dioxide, the construction of an almost infinite diversity of phases and systems is possible. Natural phases and systems may both vary almost indefinitely in number and variety of components, in concentrations, and in configurations. They may be so constituted as to produce the most varied forms of activity. Like their components they may manifest the greatest diversity of properties, and their forms may include all the possible forms of life and of the mineral kingdom.

These and many other things depend upon the properties of hydrogen, carbon, and oxygen. They make up, I cannot doubt, the most remarkable group of causes of the teleological appearance of nature. Yet it must not be forgotten that they only coöperate in the process of evolution, and that many other causes are necessary to the effects. Not only are the laws of nature concerned, but also the characteristics of the solar system, the peculiar characteristics of the earth, and especially the mysterious origin of life. Without this event the process of evolution must have remained in a far simpler condition. But, more conspicuously than the other factors in the evolutionary process, these fundamental properties of matter permit, in a very strict scientific sense, freedom of development. This freedom is, figuratively speaking, merely the freedom of trial and error. It makes possible the occurrence of a great variety of trials and a large proportion of successes. I need hardly say that we arrive at the concept of this kind of freedom only by neglecting the causes which determine the trials — in this case both general laws, and special peculiarities of our earth. But this is equivalent to the remark that we are investigating one particular aspect of a complex problem. In short we are following the invariable method of science.

The nature of the properties of the three elements which thus coöperate to bring these conditions to pass must now be examined. All properties, with the exception of a few which at present cannot be recognized as bearing upon the general characteristics of systems, are concerned. Each of these properties is almost or quite unique, either because it has a maximum or a minimum value or nearly so, among all known substances, or because

it involves a unique relationship, **or an anomaly.**
No other element or group of elements possesses
properties which on any account can be compared
with these. All such are deficient at many points,
both qualitatively or quantitatively. Moreover,
since the whole analysis is founded upon the characteristics of systems and therefore upon concepts
which according to Gibbs are independent of and
specify nothing about the properties of the elements, it is unnecessary to examine the possibility
of the existence of other groups of properties which
may be otherwise unique.

Thus we reach the conclusion that the properties
of hydrogen, carbon, and oxygen make up a unique
ensemble of properties each one of which is itself
unique. This ensemble of properties is of the
highest importance in the evolutionary process, for
it is that which makes diversity possible. To this
end it provides materials, and in large measure the
necessary stability of conditions. We have already
seen that diversity, as Spencer declared, is radically
necessary to evolution.

We may therefore conclude that there is here
revealed an order or pattern in the properties of the
elements. This new order is, so to speak, hidden,
when one considers the properties of matter
abstractly and statically, for it is recognizable and
intelligible *only* through its effects. It becomes
evident only when time is taken into consideration.

It has a dynamical significance, and relates to evolution. It is associated with the periodic system of the elements in somewhat the same way that the functional order is related to the structural order in biology. Hence it is not independent of the other order, but may be said to lie masked within it.

This is no novel experience, that the consideration of phenomena in time should lead to new points of view. From Galileo's inclined plane and pendulum to the times of Darwin and modern physical chemistry the progress of dynamics has steadily modified our outlook on nature. In truth, it might almost have been said *a priori* that a new order must be revealed by a study of the properties of matter in relation to evolution.

The unique ensemble of properties of water, carbonic acid and the three elements constitutes, among the properties of matter, the fittest ensemble of characteristics for durable mechanism. No other environment, that is to say no environment other than the surface of a planet upon which water and carbonic acid are the primary constituents, does or could so highly favor the widest range of durability and activity in the widest range of material systems — in systems varying with respect to phases, to components, and to concentrations. This environment is indeed the *fittest*. It has a claim to the use of the superlative based upon quantitative measurement and exhaustive treatment, which is altogether lacking in the case of the fitness of the organism. For the organism, so we fondly hope, is ever becoming more fit, and the law of evolution is the survival of the fitter.

Yet it is only for mechanism in general, and not for any special form of mechanism, whether life as we know it, or a steam engine, that this environment is fittest. The ocean, for example, fits mechanism in general; and, if you will, it fits the fish and the plankton diatom, though not man or a butterfly. But, of course, as everybody has known since 1859, it is really the fish and the diatom which fit the ocean. And this leads to a biological conclusion.

Just because life must manifest itself in and through mechanism, just because, being in this world, it must inhabit a more or less durable, more or less active physico-chemical system of more or less complexity in its phases, components, and concentrations, it is conditioned. The inorganic, such as it is, imposes certain conditions upon the organic. Accordingly, we may say that the special characteristics of the inorganic are the fittest for those general characteristics of the organic which the general characteristics of the inorganic impose upon the organic. This is the one side of reciprocal biological fitness. The other side may be similarly

stated: Through adaptation the special characteristics of the organic come to fit the special characteristics of a particular environment, to fit, not
any planet, but a little corner of the earth.

This is a most imperfect characterization of the
dynamic order in the properties of the elements,
for it involves only three among more than eighty
substances. Equally serious, perhaps, is the difficulty of reducing the statement to a methodical
form. We shall do well therefore to accept the
facts without seeking to elaborate a description
of them.

But the ensemble of characteristics of hydrogen,
carbon, and oxygen cannot yet be dismissed. We
have first to note that the connection of the properties of these elements is not to be disregarded
on the ground that it is an affair of the " reflective
judgment." For as we have seen that consideration would also lead to the rejection of the connection of properties described by the periodic system.
Nor can we look upon either of these peculiarities of
the matter which makes up the universe as in any
sense the work of chance, or as mere contingency.

" There is, in truth, not one chance in countless
millions of millions that the many unique properties of carbon, hydrogen, and oxygen, and especially of their stable compounds water and carbonic
acid, which chiefly make up the atmosphere of a
new planet, should simultaneously occur in the

three elements otherwise than through the operation of a natural law which somehow connects
them together. There is no greater probability
that these unique properties should be without due
(i. e. relevant) cause uniquely favorable to the
organic mechanism. These are no mere accidents;
an explanation is to seek. It must be admitted,
however, that no explanation is at hand." [1]

It is generally admitted that the coincidence
of properties itself is now open to scientific investigation. The interconnection between many particular properties has in fact been recognized
throughout the whole system of the elements, and
the periodic classification itself is founded upon
such relationships. Recent investigations have
tended to extend our knowledge of these, and to
show that many possess a truly quantitative character, as well as an intelligible explanation.[2] It is
also quite clear that elements of low atomic weight,
in addition to their tendency to become concentrated at the surface of the earth and in the atmosphere, possess certain other characteristics which
depend upon the low atomic weight itself. Among
these the most conspicuous is high specific heat.

" Be that as it may, chemical science is still a
very long way from accounting for the simultaneous occurrence of the various characteristics of

---

[1] *The Fitness of the Environment*, p. 276.

[2] Richards, *Journal of the American Chemical Society, 36,* 2417
(1914).

water, especially if we include such things as heat
of formation, solvent power, the process of hydro-
lytic cleavage, the degree of solubility of carbon
dioxide, the anomalous expansion on cooling near
the freezing point, etc.

" There is, in fact, exceedingly little ground for
hope that any single explanation of these coinci-
dences can arise from current hypotheses and laws.
But if to the coincidence of the unique properties
of water we add that of the chemical properties of
the three elements, a problem results under which
the science of today must surely break down. If
these taken as a whole are ever to be understood,
it will be in the future, when research has pene-
trated far deeper into the riddle of the properties
of matter. Nevertheless an explanation cognate
with known laws is conceivable, and in the light of
experience it would be folly to think it impossible
or even improbable." [1]

Yet such an explanation, once attained, could
little avail, because a further more difficult problem
remains. How did it come about that each and all
of these many unique properties should be favorable to the production of systems and therefore
to the process of evolution? Existing knowledge
provides no clue to an answer, for there seems to
be here no possibility of any interaction like that
involved in the production of dynamic equilibrium

[1] *The Fitness of the Environment*, pp. 277–278.

or natural selection. Yet the connection between these properties of the elements, almost infinitely improbable as the result of contingency, can only be regarded, is in truth only fully intelligible even if mechanistically explained, as a preparation for the evolutionary process. By this I mean to say that it resembles adaptation. Otherwise all our preceding scientific analysis must be devoid of real meaning. This ensemble is the condition of the production of many systems from few. Any other sensibly different distribution of the properties among the elements, almost infinitely numerous though such conceivable distributions may be, would very greatly restrict the possibilities of the multiplication of systems. In other words the possibility is negligible that conditions equally favorable to the production of diversity in the course of evolution should arise without relevant cause. But we are ignorant of the existence of any cause, except, of course, the living organism, which can thus produce results that are fully intelligible only in their relation to later events. Nevertheless we can, on no account, unless we are to abandon that principle of probability which is the basis of every scientific induction, deny this connection, in character an adaptation, between the properties of matter and the diversity of evolution.[1] For the

[1] One might go through the form of calculating the probability of this particular distribution of properties occurring among the ele-

connection is fully evident and the result is reached by a scientific demonstration.

This conclusion is so important that I will try to state the argument in its simplest form. The process of evolution consists in increase of diversity of systems and their activities, in the multiplication of physical occurrences, or, briefly, in the production of much from little. Other things being equal there is a maximum " freedom " for such evolution on account of a certain unique arrangement of unique properties of matter. The chance that this unique ensemble of properties should occur by " accident " is almost infinitely small (i. e., less than any probability which can be practically considered). The chance that each of the unit properties of the ensemble, by itself and in coöperation with the others, should " accidentally " contribute to this " freedom " a maximum increment is also almost infinitely small. Therefore there is a relevant causal connection between the properties of the elements and the " freedom " of evolution. So at least the mind of man always argues when confronted by a group of facts which are very improbable as chance occurrences *and also* peculiarly related together. But the properties of the universal elements antedate or are logically prior

ments, and of such a distribution favoring diversity in the evolutionary process. In the present state of knowledge, such a calculation could, however, possess no interest. But the order of magnitude of the probability is obvious.

to those restricted aspects of evolution which are within the scope of our present investigations and with which we are concerned. Hence we are obliged to regard this collocation of properties as in some intelligible sense a preparation [1] for the processes of planetary evolution. For we cannot imagine an interaction between the properties of hydrogen, carbon, and oxygen and any process of planetary evolution or any similar process whereby the properties of the elements as they occur throughout the whole universe should have been modified. Therefore the properties of the elements must for the present be regarded as possessing a teleological character.

It will perhaps be objected to this argument that the cause of the peculiar properties of the three elements is conceivably a simple one, such as the properties of the electron. This is perfectly true, but quite beside the point. For, whether simple or complex in origin, the teleological connection — the logical relation of the properties of the three elements to the characteristics of systems — is complex. This complex connection is almost infinitely improbable as a chance occurrence. But the properties of electrons do not produce logical connections of this kind any more than they produce the logical connections of the multiplication

[1] I know not how otherwise to say that they unaccountably precede that to which they are unquestionably related.

table, for, like the properties of electrons, such relations are changeless characteristics of the world.

Such is the one positive scientific result which I have to contribute to the teleological problem. It must not be forgotten that this concerns but a single aspect of the teleological appearance of nature. The question of the interplay of nature's laws is left just where we found it. And the accidental advantages which our earth possesses compared with other planets of the solar system, or compared with planets as they may be abstractly conceived, are not even touched upon. Yet some of the very most remarkable conditions which lead to the diversification of evolution are there involved. We have, however, examined certain of the general characteristics of all planets as they tend to appear through the influence of the properties of matter. If at this point the analysis has not been carried to a further stage, it is because we can see the possibility of almost infinite diversity in the properties of encrusted astronomical masses, while the universe seems to possess a single and unique system of chemical elements.

The result of our analysis is, therefore, nothing but an example or specimen of the scientific analysis of the order of nature. In that it is scientific it possesses two characteristics which are important to note. First it leaves the chain of mechanical determination completely unmodified.

We need take no account whatever of such logical relations of things, just as we may completely disregard the logical relations of the periodic system, when we study any of the phenomena or groups of phenomena in nature. Secondly, like all scientific conclusions, this one depends upon the principle of probability.[1]

The scientific value of this induction of the dynamic order in the properties of the elements must depend upon its results as a means to the comprehension of the possibility of diversity and stability in the products of evolution. But there is a further philosophical aspect of the conclusion which cannot be altogether disregarded.

In arriving at the scientific conclusion we have reached a position where a single peculiarity of the teleological aspect of nature can be closely perceived and scrutinized. It is now evident that the diversity of the world largely depends upon one clearly definable group of characteristics of the elements.

In order merely to make out the course of all natural phenomena, as they have actually occurred, it is quite unnecessary to understand or to take

---

[1] Cf. Newton's fourth rule of reasoning in philosophy, in which the element of probability in every induction is clearly suggested: "Propositions in experimental philosophy obtained by wide induction are to be regarded as accurate, or at least very nearly true, until phenomena or experiments show that they may be corrected or are liable to exceptions." *Principia*, Glasgow, 1871, p. 389.

account of the peculiar relations that we have discovered to exist between the properties of three elements and the characteristics of systems. But indeed, if we are only to describe phenomena as they occur, it is not even necessary to take account of the law of gravitation. When, however, the more interesting task of explaining, or, if this term be unacceptable, of generalizing the description, is seriously taken up, the employment of laws which depend upon our perceptions or judgments of the relations existing between things becomes necessary. The development of modern science has provided us with a considerable number of such laws, of which the most conspicuous besides Newton's law are the law of the conservation of mass, the law of the conservation of energy, and the law of the degradation of energy. Such laws enable us to imagine the conditions under which all phenomena may be assumed to take place, in this manner to classify events which are widely separated in time and space, and thus gradually to approach more nearly to a conception of the world in which the infinite diversity of phenomena gives place to a very large number of classes of phenomena. In establishing such a classification Newton's law and certain others have been of inestimable service: not so the most general laws, like those of conservation and the second law of thermodynamics. These are too general to be always of value for this purpose, in that they are conditions of all phenomena. They have, therefore, often been of little use in this respect, except through their influence to make scientific thought more exact and more successfully analytical.

Another function of scientific laws has been to bring about the synthesis of the several sciences into so many self-sufficient systems of thought. In this manner the sciences have become highly organized bodies of knowledge which sometimes present quite mathematical exhaustiveness, rigorousness, and elegence in the treatment of problems and which can boast in some instances of successful predictions of unknown facts. This is the rôle for which the most general laws are best fitted. A small number of them often suffice for the systematic development of large departments of science and for the deduction of many secondary principles and large numbers of facts. Newton's *Principia* is the classical example of this, but the laws of thermodynamics are now generally admitted to surpass even the fundamental postulates of Newton's mathematical analysis for such purposes.

In the course of these developments it has been found necessary to employ other concepts than laws. For the phenomena of nature are never simple, and they rarely approach near enough to simplicity to serve as crucial experiments. The case of the solar system, as recognized and employed by Newton, is the one great example of a sufficiently isolated natural experiment. But even in a modern laboratory the man of science must always content himself with an imperfect elimination of disturbing factors. As a result of this difficulty the purely abstract ideas of mass, system, and many others have found their place in scientific thought. Thus all abstract scientific thought has come to move in an ideal world, which never corresponds exactly with reality, but which may be made to approximate to reality within any desired limits. Such are the most important functions of the abstract principles and concepts of science in so far as they now concern us.

It has been above demonstrated how the concept of system may be employed in the methodical description of the general characteristics of terrestrial evolution. And it was there pointed out that the one serious attempt to give a full description of this process, as it appears in Spencer's *Synthetic Philosophy*, is guided throughout by a vague and inaccurate anticipation of the necessary concept. Moreover, we can now see that a recognition of the peculiarities of hydrogen, carbon, and oxygen is a further means to the explanation of the process. For these peculiarities must be regarded as significant conditions of every stage, so that without them the most general characteristics of nature could never have arisen. This generalization is therefore a typical instrument of scientific thought, in that it facilitates abstract discriminations and descriptions, and helps to make possible a generalized conception of the process as a whole.

The consideration of such well-known principles of the philosophy of science would be quite out of place were it not for the teleological implications of our conclusion that the peculiarities of the elements appear to be original characteristics of the universe, or, if not, that they at least appear to arise invariably and universally when conditions make possible the stability of the atoms, and that they possess an intricate pattern, the perfect integrity of which is essential to a high degree of diversity in evolution. Nothing is more certain than that the properties of hydrogen, carbon, and oxygen are changeless throughout time and space. It is conceivable that the atoms may be formed and that they may decay. But while they exist they are uniform, or at least they possess perfect statistical uniformity which leads to absolute constancy of all their sensible characteristics, that is to say of all the properties with which we are concerned. And yet this original peculiarity of things is the chief cause of diversity in the stage of the evolutionary process which is fully within the grasp of natural science.

But it may be objected that in the strict scientific sense this is not a relation of cause and effect

at all. What we are concerned with is an indefinite
number of chains of causation in each of which the
preceding condition is at every point the cause of,
i. e. that which unequivocally determines, the
succeeding condition. Like Newton's law, or any
other principle of science, great or small, the
peculiarities of the three elements are a cause of
nothing. They are merely the conditions under
which the phenomena reveal themselves. And
the world is now what it is because it was something else just a moment ago. There can be no
objection to this position as one convenient way
of conceiving the world. But if it is supposed that
we are therefore required summarily to close our
inquiry the reply must be made that we shall then
have to exclude all the laws of nature from our
philosophy.

Accordingly we may return to the conclusion
that the principal peculiarity of the universe
which makes diversity of evolution possible is
original and anterior to all instances of the processes which it conditions. And we may recall the
fact that this peculiarity consists of a group of
characteristics such that they cannot be regarded as
merely contingent. Finally, it will be remembered
that *the relation of this group of properties to the
characteristics of systems is also such that it cannot be
merely contingent.* I believe these statements to be
scientific facts. If this be so we have arrived at the

solution for a special case of Aristotle's problem of "the character of the material nature whose necessary results have been made available by rational nature for a final cause."

Of course objections will at once arise to the terms *rational nature* and *final cause*. In reply I have little to say beyond what has been developed in the historical introduction to this Essay. It was for the purpose of discovering, if possible, in what sense such terms may be allowed in the thought of our times that the introduction was written. In the first place I believe that the term *rational nature* of the fourth century B.C. may be translated into the modern term *laws of nature*. For these laws are exclusively rational. They are the product of the human reason, and are not conceived by science to have objective existence in nature. And this is clearly true of the *relation* between the properties of the elements and the characteristics of systems. Secondly, as we have seen above, all phenomena are phenomena of systems. Hence the operations of a final cause, if such there be, can only occur through the evolution of systems. Therefore the greatest possible freedom for the evolution of systems involves the greatest possible freedom for the operations of a final cause.

The above statement may now be modified to the following effect: We possess a solution for a special case of the problem of the characteristics of the material nature whose necessary results have been made available by the laws of nature for any hypothetical final cause. Thus the whole problem of the teleological significance of our scientific investigation reduces to the simple but infinitely difficult question whether a final cause is to be postulated.

Here we are once more confronted by the fact that no mechanical cause of the properties of the elements except an antecedent process is conceivable. But, since the elements are uniform throughout space, there cannot have been, in the proper sense, any contingency about the operation of this cause. At the most, contingency can have produced nothing but an irregular distribution of the different elements in different parts of the universe. Moreover, according to the orthodox scientific view, there is no room for contingency in such discussions. Accordingly the properties of the elements are to be regarded as fully determined from the earliest conceivable epoch and perfectly changeless in time. This we may take as a postulate.[1] In like manner the abstract characteristics

[1] On this point the experimental evidence of astronomical spectrum analysis is available, and there seems to be no escape from the conclusion that hydrogen and the other elements whose spectra we thus detect possess the same properties throughout the universe. These appear to be independent of the age and temperature of the star in which they occur. It is also known that meteoric iron has the

of systems must also be regarded as fully determined and absolutely changeless in time. This is a second postulate.

Finally, the relation between the numerous properties of hydrogen, carbon, and oxygen, severally and in coöperation (relatively to the same relation between the properties of all the other elements) and the necessary conditions of existence of systems in respect of number, diversity, and durability, as these conditions are defined by the exact analysis of Willard Gibbs, is not merely contingent. In other words the statistical probability that this connection has a relevant cause (i. e. relevant to the evolutionary process) is greater than the statistical probability which we can ever reasonably demand or generally realize in the establishment of the principles and facts of science.

It may be recalled that we are here dealing with three elements among more than eighty, and with more than twenty of their properties. It must also be remembered that this is not merely a question of the probability of the coincidence of the unique properties among the three elements, but especially of the *relation* of these properties regarded as an ensemble to the properties of systems. The

same atomic weight and in general the same properties as terrestrial iron. For a careful consideration of such questions, cf. Richards, Faraday Lecture, *Journal of the Chemical Society* (London), *99*, 1201, 1911.

uniqueness of the properties is significant because it fully proves their unique *fitness* for systems. If it should appear that these properties are the result of one simple cause the question would become: what is the probability that from a single cause this ensemble of unique fitnesses for a subsequent process should arise ? But according to Gibbs the relevant conditions of this process are independent of the properties of the elements and of their compounds. This problem is therefore mathematically identical with the preceding form of the question.

No mechanical cause of the properties of the elements is, accordingly, conceivable which should be mechanically dependent upon the characteristics of systems. For no *mechanical* cause whatever is conceivable of those original conditions, whatever they may be, which unequivocally determine the changeless properties of the elements and the general characteristics of systems alike. We are therefore led to the hypothesis that the properties of the three elements are somehow a preparation for the evolutionary process. In truth this is the only explanation of the connection which is at present imaginable. For we have recognized a pattern in the properties of the elements and as a pattern this is only to be described in relation to the diversity of evolution.

Such an hypothesis will have to be judged on its merits. Admitting the scientific facts, it possesses, so far as I can see, two defects. In the first place the term preparation is scientifically unintelligible. Secondly, this hypothesis is not only novel, but it is different in kind from all recognized scientific hypotheses.[1] For no other scientific hypothesis involves preparations except those which originate in the organism. In short we are face to face with the problem of Design.

Concerning the philosophical aspects of this question I have nothing new to say. It seems to me clearly established in the history of thought that when this problem arises the only safety is to be found in retreat and in employing the vaguest possible term which can be imagined, from which all implication of design or purpose has been completely eliminated. By common consent that term has come to be recognized as *teleology*. Thus we say that adaptation is teleological, but do not say that it is the result of design or purpose. I shall therefore modify the above statement and assert that the connection between the properties of the three elements and the evolutionary process is teleological and non-mechanical.

But it will still be asked if this new statement has any intelligible meaning. The answer is

[1] Except guesses about the origin of life, in that these involve the origin of organization.

affirmative. For biological organization is teleological and non-mechanical.[1] Yet, as we have
seen, the concept of organization is now in general
scientific use. How then should it be thought
strange to find in the inorganic world something
slightly analogous to that which is clearly recognized in the organic? Indeed no idea is older
or more common than a suspicion that somehow
nature itself is a great imperfect organism. There
is nothing in such a view to commend it to natural
science. But there may well be a foundation in
undefined realities vaguely perceived.

We thus reach the conclusion that in one most
important respect the teleological appearance of
nature depends upon an unquestionable relationship between certain original characteristics of the

[1] It may be recalled that organization consists in a teleological and
non-mechanical relationship between mechanical things and processes.
In both cases the relationship is rational and non-mechanical, the
things related mechanical and non-rational. Or, in other words, the
relation is an affair of the " reflective judgment," the things related of
the " determinant judgment." It is the failure to understand this distinction which is at the bottom of most controversies concerning biological teleology. The understanding may be facilitated by noting
that the periodic classification also involves a rational and non-mechanical relation. This analysis must not be pressed too far, however.
For while it would suffice as an explanation of the periodic system to
demonstrate the relation of the periodic properties to the properties of
electrons, such a demonstration would not suffice for our present purposes, because it could not account for the relation between the properties of the elements and the independent requirements of systems.
This *connection* is the teleological factor in the present problem, and it
is an original changeless property of the universe.

universe which, because it is *merely* a relationshp
and in no sense a mechanical connection, because
it is unmodified by the evolutionary process and
changeless in time, is to be described as teleological. The reason why it must be described as
teleological is that there is no other word to
describe it.[1] It is teleological just as the periodic
system is periodic. In other words, the appearance of harmonious unities in nature, which no man
can escape, depends upon a genuine harmonious
unity that is proved to exist among certain of the
abstract changeless characteristics of the universe.
As a qualification of such abstract characteristics,
contingency, which is the one concept opposed to
harmonious unity of nature, finds no place.

Thus, at length, with the help of the scientific
analysis, the result which was above declared to be
necessary for a belief in teleology [2] is attained. For
the teleology of nature is recognized through a
connection, conceivable only as teleological, among
nature's laws, i. e. among the general abstract
characteristics of nature which may be exactly
defined.

It must not be forgotten that there is here
involved but a single instance of a teleological
connection between abstract characteristics of

---

[1] *Harmonious* and *organic* seem not quite to meet the point, but it
must be remembered that design and purpose are not in question.

[2] Above, p. 117.

nature. Though we can vaguely distinguish other teleological aspects of the laws of nature, as in the tendency toward dynamic equilibrium, there seems to be at present no possibility of investigating the problem in a more general manner. Thus we cannot judge how far they may be all thus linked together. Yet this simple result is sufficient greatly to strengthen a philosophical conclusion which many thoughtful men have reached from the most varied experiences.

Charles Darwin has stated his own opinion as follows: " Another source of conviction in the existence of God, connected with the reason, and not with the feelings, impresses me as having much more weight. This follows from the extreme difficulty or rather impossibility of conceiving this immense and wonderful universe, including man with his capacity of looking far backwards and far into futurity, as the result of blind chance or necessity. When thus reflecting I feel compelled to look to a First Cause having an intelligent mind in some degree analogous to that of man; and I deserve to be called a Theist. This conclusion was strong in my mind about the time, as far as I can remember, when I wrote the ' Origin of Species,' and it is since that time that it has very gradually, with many fluctuations, become weaker. But then arises the doubt, can the mind of man, which has, as I fully believe, been developed from a mind as low as that possessed by the lowest animals, be trusted when it draws such general conclusions ?

" I cannot pretend to throw the least light on such abstruse problems. The mystery of the beginnings of all things is insoluble by us; and I for one must be content to remain an Agnostic." [1]

Evidently Darwin's unmethodical consideration of the problem developed from an original theological view to a vague theism, and from this to a hesitating denial of the possibility that any intelligible explanation of the teleology of nature can be found. Design and purpose he cannot admit, but from the teleology of nature itself he could not escape. In our own times thousands of thoughtful men have passed through these same phases of speculation. But this position is identical with that systematically established by Hume and accepted by a long line of other philosophers. As Cournot perceived, the tormenting riddle, eternal and inexplicable, is the existence, not of the universe, but of nature.

The whole history of thought does but prove the justice of this conclusion. We may progressively lay bare the order of nature and define it with the aid of the exact sciences. Thus we may recognize it for what it is, and now at length we clearly see that it is teleological. But we shall never find the

[1] *Life and Letters of Charles Darwin*, London, 1888, Vol. I, pp. 312–313.

explanation of the riddle, for it concerns the origin of things. Upon this subject clear ideas and close reasoning are no longer possible, for thought has arrived at one of its natural frontiers. Nothing more remains but to admit that the riddle surpasses us and to conclude that the contrast of mechanism with teleology is the very foundation of the order of nature,[1] which must ever be regarded from two complementary points of view, as a vast assemblage of changing systems, and as an harmonious unity of changeless laws and qualities working together in the process of evolution.

This conclusion rests upon an analysis which may now be recapitulated in its most summary form.

First, the characteristics of systems (phases, components, activities, etc.) are universal conditions of all phenomena, except the infra-molecular. They do not depend upon the peculiarities of the numerous varieties of matter, and they are changeless.

Secondly, the properties of matter are so distributed among the elements that three elements possess a unique ensemble of unique characteristics, — maxima, minima, and other singular properties. But this pattern in the properties of matter is also a universal condition of phenomena. It seems to

[1] Above, p. 114.

be quite unmodified by the characteristics of systems, in that, like such characteristics, it is changeless.

Therefore we cannot conceive these two abstract qualities of the universe as dependent, in any physical sense, upon each other. Conceived by Gibbs to be originally independent, they are alike unmodified in time. It is therefore at present impossible to imagine that there should be, in the mathematical sense, a functional relationship between them. But the properties of the three elements lead to maximum freedom of the evolutionary process in all respects conceivable by physical science. So far as the known properties of matter are concerned, considering them both quantitatively and qualitatively, every other sensibly different distribution of the properties among the elements would involve great restrictions. Thus conditions are actually established (relatively to other imaginable arrangements of the properties of matter) for the existence of the greatest possible number, diversity and duration of systems, phases, components, and activities. So it comes about that, in every physical respect, the process of evolution is free to produce more rather than less.

There is involved in this conclusion no judgment of value, for the whole discussion depends simply upon the ability to distinguish inequalities.

It cannot be that the nature of this relationship is, like organic adaptations, mechanically conditioned. For relationships are mechanically conditioned in a significant manner only when there is opportunity for modification through interaction. But here the things related are supposed to be changeless in time, or, in short, absolute properties of the universe.

According to the theory of probabilities this connection between the properties of matter and the process of evolution cannot be due to mere contingency. Therefore, since the physico-chemical functional relationship is not in question, there must be admitted a functional relationship of another kind, somewhat like that known to physiology. This functional relationship can only be described as teleological.

APPENDIX

CLERK MAXWELL ON DETERMINISM AND FREE WILL [1]

Does the progress of Physical Science tend to give any advantage to the opinion of Necessity (or Determinism) over that of the Contingency of Events and the Freedom of the Will?

11th FEBRUARY 1873.

THE general character and tendency of human thought is a topic the interest of which is not confined to professional philosophers. Though every one of us must, each for himself, accept some sort of a philosophy, good or bad, and though the whole virtue of this philosophy depends on it being our own, yet none of us thinks it out entirely for himself. It is essential to our comfort that we should know whether we are going with the general stream of human thought or against it, and if it should turn out that the general stream flows in a direction different from the current of our private thought, though we may endeavour to explain it as the result of a wide-spread aberration of intel-

---

[1] Reprinted from *The Life of James Clerk Maxwell*, by Lewis Campbell and William Garnett, London, 1882, pp 434–444.

lect, we would be more satisfied if we could obtain some evidence that it is not ourselves who are going astray.

In such an enquiry we need some fiducial point or standard of reference, by which we may ascertain the direction in which we are drifting. The books written by men of former ages who thought about the same questions would be of great use, if it were not that we are apt to derive a wrong impression from them if we approach them by a course of reading unknown to those for whom they were written.

There are certain questions, however, which form the *pièces de résistance* of philosophy, on which men of all ages have exhausted their arguments, and which are perfectly certain to furnish matter of debate to generations to come, and which may therefore serve to show how we are drifting. At a certain epoch of our adolescence those of us who are good for anything begin to get anxious about these questions, and unless the cares of this world utterly choke our metaphysical anxieties, we become developed into advocates of necessity or of free-will. What it is which determines for us which side we shall take must for the purpose of this essay be regarded as contingent. According to Mr. F. Galton, it is derived from structureless elements in our parents, which were probably never developed in their earthly existence, and which may have been handed down to them, still in the latent state, through untold generations. Much might be said in favour of such a congenital bias towards a particular scheme of philosophy; at the same time we must acknowledge that much of a man's mental history depends upon events occurring after his birth in time, and that he is on the whole more likely to espouse doctrines which harmonise with the particular set of ideas to which he is induced, by the process of education, to confine his attention. What will be the probable effect if these ideas happen mainly to be those of modern physical science ?

The intimate connexion between physical and metaphysical science is indicated even by their names. What are the chief requisites of a physical laboratory ? Facilities for measuring space, time, and mass. What is the occupation of a metaphysician ? Speculating on the modes of difference of coexistent things, on invariable sequences, and on the existence of matter.

He is nothing but a physicist disarmed of all his weapons, — a disembodied spirit trying to measure distances in terms of his own cubit, to form a chronology in which intervals of time are measured by the number of thoughts which they include, and to evolve a standard pound out of his own self-consciousness. Taking metaphysicians singly, we find again that as is their physics, so is their metaphysics. Descartes, with his perfect insight into geometrical truth, and his wonderful ingenuity in the imagination of mechanical contrivances, was far behind the other great men of his time with respect to the conception of matter as a receptacle of momentum and energy. His doctrine of the collision of bodies is ludicrously absurd. He admits, indeed, that the facts are against him, but explains them as the result either of the want of perfect hardness in the bodies, or of the action of the surrounding air. His inability to form that notion which we now call force is exemplified in his explanation of the hardness of bodies as the result of the quiescence of their parts.

"Neque profecto ullum glutinum possumus excogitare, quod particulas durorum corporum firmius inter se conjungat, quàm ipsarum quies." *Princip., Pars* II. LV.

Descartes, in fact, was a firm believer that matter has but one essential property, namely extension, and his influence in preserving this pernicious heresy in existence extends even to very recent times. Spinoza's idea of matter, as he receives it from the authorities, is exactly that of Descartes; and if he has added to it another essential function, namely thought, the new ingredient does not interfere with the old, and certainly does not bring the matter of Descartes into closer resemblance with that of Newton.

The influence of the physical ideas of Newton on philosophical thought deserves a careful study. It may be traced in a very direct way through Maclaurin and the Stewarts to the Scotch School, the members of which had all listened to the popular expositions of the Newtonian Philosophy in their respective colleges. In England, Boyle and Locke reflect Newtonian ideas with tolerable distinctness, though both have ideas of their own. Berkeley, on the other hand, though he is a master of the language of his time, is quite impervious to its ideas. Samuel Clarke is perhaps one of the best examples of the influence of Newton; while Roger Cotes, in spite of his clever exposition of Newton's doctrines, must be condemned as one of the earliest heretics bred in the bosom of Newtonianism.

It is absolutely manifest from these and other instances that any development of physical science is likely to produce some modification of the methods and ideas of philosophers, provided that the physical ideas are expounded in such a way that the philosophers can understand them.

The principal developments of physical ideas in modern times have been —

1st. The idea of matter as the receptacle of momentum and energy. This we may attribute to Galileo and some of his contemporaries. This idea is fully expressed by Newton, under the form of Laws of Motion.

2d. The discussion of the relation between the fact of gravitation and the maxim that matter cannot act where it is not.

3d. The discoveries in Physical Optics, at the beginning of this century. These have produced much less effect outside the scientific world than might be expected. There are two reasons for this. In the first place it is difficult, especially in these days of the separation of technical from popular knowledge, to expound physical optics to persons not professedly mathematicians. The second reason is, that it is extremely easy to show such persons the phenomena, which are very beautiful in themselves, and this is often accepted as instruction in physical optics.

4th. The development of the doctrine of the Conservation of Energy. This has produced a far greater effect on the thinking world outside that of technical thermodynamics.

As the doctrine of the conservation of matter gave a definiteness to statements regarding the immateriality of the soul, so the doctrine of the conservation of energy, when applied to living beings, leads to the conclusion that the soul of an animal is not, like the mainspring of a watch, the motive power of the body, but that its function is rather that of a steersman of a vessel, — not to produce, but to regulate and direct the animal powers.

5th. The discoveries in Electricity and Magnetism labour under the same disadvantages as those in Light. It is difficult to present the ideas in an adequate manner to laymen, and it is easy to show them wonderful experiments.

6th. On the other hand, recent developments of Molecular Science seem likely to have a powerful effect on the world of thought. The doctrine that visible bodies apparently at rest are made up of parts, each of which is moving with the velocity of a cannon ball, and yet never departing to a visible extent from its mean place, is sufficiently startling to attract the attention of an unprofessional man.

But I think the most important effect of molecular science on our way of thinking will be that it forces on our attention the distinction between two kinds of knowledge, which we may call for convenience the Dynamical and Statistical.

The statistical method of investigating social questions has Laplace for its most scientific and Buckle for its most popular expounder. Persons are grouped according to some characteristic, and the number of persons forming the group is set down under that characteristic. This is the raw material from which the statist endeavours to deduce general theorems in sociology. Other students of human nature proceed on a different plan. They observe individual men, ascertain their history, analyse their motives, and compare their expectation of what they will do with their actual conduct. This may be called the dynamical method of study as applied to man. However imperfect the dynamical study of man may be in practice, it evidently is the only perfect method in principle, and its shortcomings arise from the limitation of our powers rather than from a faulty method of procedure. If we betake ourselves to the statistical method, we do so confessing that we are unable to follow the details of each individual case, and expecting that the effects of widespread causes, though very different in each individual, will produce an average result on the whole nation, from a study of which we may estimate the character and propensities of an imaginary being called the Mean Man.

Now, if the molecular theory of the constitution of bodies is true, all our knowledge of matter is of the statistical kind. A constituent molecule of a body has properties very different from those of the body to which it belongs. Besides its immutability and other recondite properties, it has a velocity which is different from that which we attribute to the body as a whole.

The smallest portion of a body which we can discern consists of a vast number of such molecules, and all that we can learn about this group of molecules is statistical information. We can determine the motion of the centre of gravity of the group, but not that of any one of its members for the time being, and these members themselves are continually passing from one group to another in a manner confessedly beyond our power of tracing them.[1]

Hence those uniformities which we observe in our experiments with quantities of matter containing millions of millions of molecules are uniformities of the same kind as those explained by Laplace and wondered at by Buckle, arising from the slumping together of multitudes of cases, each of which is by no means uniform with the others.

The discussion of statistical matter is within the province of human reason, and valid consequences may be deduced from it by legitimate methods; but there are certain peculiarities in the very form of the results which indicate that they belong to a different department of knowledge from the domain of exact science. They are not symmetrical functions of the time. It makes all the difference in the world whether we suppose the enquiry to be historical or prophetical — whether our object is to deduce the past state or the future state of things from the known present state. In astronomy, the two problems differ only in the sign of t, the time; in the theory of the diffusion of matter, heat, or motion, the prophetical problem is always capable of solution; but the historical one,

---

[1] This paragraph could not, of course, be written today.

except in singular cases, is insoluble. There may be other cases in which the past, but not the future, may be deducible from the present. Perhaps the process by which we remember past events, by submitting our memory to analysis, may be a case of this kind.

Much light may be thrown on some of these questions by the consideration of stability and instability. When the state of things is such that an infinitely small variation of the present state will alter only by an infinitely small quantity the state at some future time, the condition of the system, whether at rest or in motion, is said to be stable; but when an infinitely small variation in the present state may bring about a finite difference in the state of the system in a finite time, the condition of the system is said to be unstable.

It is manifest that the existence of unstable conditions renders impossible the prediction of future events, if our knowledge of the present state is only approximate, and not accurate.

It has been well pointed out by Professor Balfour Stewart that physical stability is the characteristic of those systems from the contemplation of which determinists draw their arguments, and physical stability [instability] that of those living bodies, and moral instability that of those developable souls, which furnish to consciousness the conviction of free will.

Having thus pointed out some of the relations of physical science to the question, we are the better prepared to enquire what is meant by determination and what by free will.

No one, I suppose, would assign to free will a more than infinitesimal range. No leopard can change his spots, nor can any one by merely wishing it, or, as some say, *willing* it, introduce discontinuity into his course of existence. Our free will at the best is like that of Lucretius's atoms, — which at quite uncertain times and places deviate in an uncertain manner from their course. In the course of this our mortal life we more or less frequently find ourselves on a physical or moral watershed, where an imperceptible deviation is sufficient to determine into which of two valleys we shall descend. The doctrine of free will asserts that in some such cases the Ego alone is the determining cause. The doctrine of Determinism asserts that in every case, without exception, the result is determined by the previous conditions of the subject, whether bodily or mental, and that Ego is mistaken in supposing himself in any way the cause of the actual result, as both what he is pleased to call decisions and the resultant action are corresponding events due to the same fixed laws. Now, when we speak of causes and effects, we always imply some person who knows the causes and deduces the effects. Who is this person? Is he a man, or is he the Deity?

If he is man, — that is to say, a person who can make observations with a certain finite degree of accuracy, — we have seen that it is only in certain cases that he can predict results with even approximate correctness.

If he is the Deity, I object to any argument founded on a supposed acquaintance with the conditions of Divine foreknowledge.

The subject of the essay is the relation to determinism, not of theology, metaphysics, or mathematics, but of physical science, — the science which depends for its material on the observation and measurement of visible things, but which aims at the development of doctrines whose consistency with each other shall be apparent to our reason.

It is a metaphysical doctrine that from the same antecedents follow the same consequents. No one can gainsay this. But it is not of much use in a world like this, in which the same antecedents never again concur, and nothing ever happens twice. Indeed, for aught we know, one of the antecedents might be the precise date and place of the event, in which case experience would go for nothing. The metaphysical axiom would be of use only to a being possessed of the knowledge of contingent events, *scientia simplicis intelligentiæ*, — a degree of knowledge to which mere omniscience of all facts, *scientia visionis*, is but ignorance.

The physical axiom which has a somewhat similar aspect is "That from like antecedents follow like consequents." But here we have passed from sameness to likeness, from absolute accuracy to a more or less rough approximation. There are certain classes of phenomena, as I have said, in which a small error in the data only introduces a small error in the result. Such are, among others, the larger phenomena of the Solar System, and those in which the more elementary laws in Dynamics contribute the greater part of the result. The course of events in these cases is stable.

There are other classes of phenomena which are more complicated, and in which cases of instability may occur, the number of such cases increasing, in an exceedingly rapid manner, as the number of variables increases. Thus, to take a case from a branch of science which comes next to astronomy itself as a manifestation of order: In the refraction of light, the direction of the refracted ray depends on that of the incident ray, so that in general, if the one direction be slightly altered, the other also will be slightly altered. In doubly refracting media there are two refracting rays, but it is true of each of them that like causes produce like effects. But if the direction of the ray within a biaxal crystal is nearly but not exactly coincident with that of the ray-axis of the crystal, a small change in direction will produce a great change in the direction of the emergent ray. Of course, this arises from a singularity in the properties of the ray-axis, and there are only two ray-axes among the infinite number of possible directions of lines in the crystal; but it is to be expected that in phenomena of higher complexity there will be a far greater number of singularities, near which the axiom about like causes producing like effects ceases to be true. Thus the conditions under which gun-cotton explodes are far from being well known; but the aim of chemists is not so much to predict the time at which gun-cotton will go off of itself, as to find a kind of gun-cotton which, when placed in certain circumstances, has never yet exploded, and this even when slight irregularities both in the manufacture and in the storage are taken account of by trying numerous and long continued experiments.

In all such cases there is one common circumstance, — the system has a quantity of potential energy, which is capable of being transformed into motion, but which cannot begin to be so transformed till the system has reached a certain configuration, to attain which requires an expenditure of work, which in certain cases may be infinitesimally small, and in general bears no definite proportion to the energy developed in consequence thereof. For example, the rock loosed by frost and balanced on a singular point of the mountain-side, the little spark which kindles the great forest, the little word which sets the world a fighting, the little scruple which prevents a man from doing his will, the little spore which blights all the potatoes, the little gemmule which makes us philosophers or idiots. Every existence above a certain rank has its singular points: the higher the rank, the more of them. At these points, influences whose physical magnitude is too small to be taken account of by a finite being, may produce results of the greatest importance. All great results produced by human endeavour depend on taking advantage of these singular states when they occur.

> There is a tide in the affairs of men
> Which, taken at the flood, leads on to fortune.

The man of tact says, " the right word at the right time," and, " a word spoken in due season how good is it ! " The man of no tact is like vinegar upon nitre when he sings his songs to a heavy heart. The ill-timed admonition hardens the heart, and the good resolution, taken when it is sure to be broken, becomes macadamised into pavement for the abyss.

It appears then that in our own nature there are more singular points, — where prediction, except from absolutely perfect data, and guided by the omniscience of contingency, becomes impossible, — than there are in any lower organisation. But singular points are by their very nature isolated, and from no appreciable fraction of the continuous course of our existence. Hence predictions of human conduct may be made in many cases. First, with respect to those who have no character at all, especially when considered in crowds, after the statistical method. Second, with respect to individuals of confirmed character, with respect to actions of the kind for which their character is confirmed.

If, therefore, those cultivators of physical science from whom the intelligent public deduce their conception of the physicist, and whose style is recognised as marking with a scientific stamp the doctrines they promulgate, are led in pursuit of the arcana of science to the study of the singularities and instabilities, rather than the continuities and stabilities of things, the promotion of natural knowledge may tend to remove that prejudice in favour of determinism which seems to arise from assuming that the physical science of the future is a mere magnified image of that of the past.

FECHNER ON THE TENDENCY TO STABILITY[1]

Let us consider any assemblage of material particles, under the action of forces of any kind within a limited space, the system being abstracted from external influences, or subjected to the action of constant external influences, and the operation of the freedom of the will being either absent or impossible. Then, given any original positions, velocities, and directions of the particles, all the succeeding states of the system will be determined by the original conditions. Now if there are among these conditions such that they originally constitute or in the course of the movements produce a state to which after a given time the system must again return, then the system will continue to change until, among all possible states, which can be passed through in the circumstances, that very one has been established which is involved in the determination of a return; until then the system can, so to speak, have no rest. Meanwhile the original movements, which are arbitrarily conceived as changing in form and in velocity, and which involve changes in the positions of the particles, must have gone on, unless they immediately condition a state of periodicity.

[1] *Einige Ideen zur Schöpfungs-und Entwickelungsgeschichte der Organismen,* von Gustav Theodor Fechner, Leipzig, 1873, Chapter III.

But when after a certain time the return to an earlier configuration has taken place, this same configuration must again return after the same interval, and so on indefinitely, for the same conditions are repeatedly present. These conditions determine the whole course of the movement until the next return. Accordingly the whole course of the process must repeat itself, and every phase must return in its due order. With this condition complete stability of the system is established, and can be disturbed only by a changing external influence, which is assumed to be absent.

From general considerations it may be believed, although not rigorously proved, that the disposition of any isolated material system to assume a regular internal arrangement of its parts and a regular external form is related to the principle of the tendency to stability.

INDEX

Activity, 172–175; chemical, 173, 174; defined, 129, 130.
Adaptability, iii.
Adaptation, iii, 77, 78; Darwin on, 77.
Aquinas, Thomas, 27.
Archimedes, 19, 22.
Aristotle, 10–21, 22, 23, 24, 26, 27, 28, 31, 32, 36, 37, 38, 40, 43, 52, 55, 64, 67, 73, 75, 76, 76 n, 84, 115, 116, 200; on causation, 14, 15; on organization, 16, 17, 18, 21; on teleology, 10–21.

Babbage, Charles, 38.
Bacon, Francis, 23–27, 53, 64, 75; on causation, 23–27; on teleology, 25, 26.
Bacon, Roger, 22.
Baer, K. E. von, 74–77; on organization, 76.
Bancroft, W. D., 138 n.
Behavior, 84.
Bergson, H., 105.
Berkeley, G., 92.
Bernard, Claude, 76, 77.
Bichat, M. F. X., 76.
Biology, 69–106; Aristotle on, 13–18.
Blumenbach, J. F., 63.
Bosanquet, B., 106, 112–114.
Boussinesq, V. J., 100–102, 103.
Boutroux, Emile, 102.
Butler, Joseph, 46.

Cannon, W. B., 80, 83.
Carbohydrates, 161, 162.

Carbon dioxide, solubility of, 168, 169.
Carbonic acid, acidity of, 169–171.
Carnot, N. L. Sadi, 67, 105, 146.
Cassirer, E., 38 n.
Causation, Aristotle on, 14, 15; F. Bacon on, 23–27; Descartes on, 29, 30; Kant on, 58, 60, 61; Leibniz on, 33–36; Newton on, 28, 65; mechanical, 28–31, 90, 91.
Causes, final. See Teleology.
Chemical activity, 173, 174.
Circulation, of water, 164, 165, 166.
Classification, of organic chemistry, 159–161.
Colloids, 171, 172.
Components, 155–167; defined, 128.
Compounds, chemical, 155–164.
Comte, Auguste, 73.
Concentration, 168–171; in systems, 130.
Conditions, of life, 7, 186, 187, 190.
Conductivity, thermal, 178, 179.
Configuration, in systems, 131.
Contingency, 102, 201, 211.
Cournot, Augustin, 102, 102 n, 107–109, 111, 116, 208; on nature, 107–109.
Couturat, Louis, 38 n.
Cusa, Nicholas of, 22.
Cuvier, G., 73, 76, 82.
Cuvier's Law, 73.

Daly, R. A., 141 n.
Darwin, C., 50, 59, 74, 77, 78, 89,